"Beads: A Memoir about Falling Apart and Putting Yourself Back Together Again is an honest and moving story of survival and renewal. Brooks takes us on a powerful and insightful journey culminating with inspiring and meaningful life-changing lessons."

— C. J. Foster
Author of *The Gardener's Daughter*

"'Everyone needs a bestie,' advises Rachael Brooks. And a 'bestie' she will become to all who have the good fortune of reading Beads, Brooks' powerful and intensely personal story of sexual assault and healing. With a rare and wonderful voice that is all at once strong and vulnerable, unvarnished and comforting, irreverent and wise, Brooks invites and welcomes us all to walk beside her on her journey and mission of making a difference. In courageously sharing her compelling story, Brooks reminds us that we each have the power to let our voices be heard and secure safer futures for entire communities. What a gift!"

— Leigh Duque
Executive Director of the Family Violence Prevention Center, Inc., DBA InterAct

Praise for Beads

"In her memoir, *Beads*, Rachael Brooks invites you to accompany her on a hero's journey she never asked for. A young woman filled with career and relationship possibilities, she is brutally raped on the edges of Washington, DC, one summer night and for the next four years must figure out her new normal. While navigating horrific obstacles, she is also bolstered by love, trust, and acts of grace. You won't easily forget Brooks's haunting images and sharp humor, which shapes this honest look of how trauma can bend, but not break, a human being. Perfectly paced and full of suspense, Beads grips you from the beginning and won't let you go."

— Alice Osborn
Author of *Heroes without Capes*

"It's seldom one has the opportunity to read a book with painfully raw details written with such candor and vulnerability. Yet Rachael Brooks writes her memoir, Beads, in a way that makes this terrible trauma accessible, meaningful, and memorable. We hear and watch news accounts of #MeToo stories. But Brooks' book ensures you deeply feel what it's like to be a victim of sexual assault. There is much to learn from her story. I highly recommend this book. It will stay within you as a stark reminder of the reality of these events, frustrating aftermath, and the bravery and perseverance involved in 'putting yourself back together again.'"

— Dee Stribling
Writer & Poet; Hillsborough, NC's 2018-2020 Poet Laureate

Beads

*A Memoir about Falling Apart and
Putting Yourself Back Together Again*

by Rachael Brooks

ISBN 978-1-63393-966-0

Published by

köehlerbooks™

210 60th Street
Virginia Beach, VA 23451
800−435−4811
www.koehlerbooks.com

Beads

Rachael Brooks

VIRGINIA BEACH
CAPE CHARLES

Dedication

To D, T, L, J, S, C, M, D, K, and A:

Your love and support have changed my life in ways you will never know.

I love you all.

To all of my fellow survivors, both known and unknown, I am so proud of you.

You are stronger than you think. Together, we will make a difference.

Table of Contents

Preface

Someone wise once said to write what you know. I was raped when I was twenty-two. My journey over the past eleven years is what I know, so I decided to write about it. I had this horrible thing happen to me, but there is beauty in how it shaped me into the person I am today.

In this day and age, it seems that people want to be heard more than ever. Whether it is in the form of national rallies or letters to your local congressmen, people are speaking out. It could be the media talking at us constantly, but I believe more voices are coming forward, more courage is being displayed, and more change is happening. The #MeToo #movement against sexual harassment and sexual assault was waged in 2017. And what a shock it was. Was this real? Was this actually happening? Women were coming forward after years and years of silence. It was shocking— and powerful. This movement was at the forefront of basically every news source out there. But also, how sick. How sad. How frustrating. These women never reported what happened to them, or, if they did, nothing was done about it. Recent statistics show that in the United States alone, one in three women and one in six men are survivors of sexual violence.[1] Quite disturbing. It all hit way too close to home, reminding me of a familiar story: sadly, the one about me nine years prior.

I had several people ask me, "How are you doing with all of this *Me Too* stuff?" Well, let's see; I wasn't jumping for joy, clearly. I was jumping,

---

1   Smith, S. G., Chen, J., Basile, K. C., Gilbert, L. K., Merrick, M. T., Patel, N., … Jain, A. (2017). The National Intimate Partner and Sexual Violence Survey (NISVS): 2010-2012 state report. Retrieved from the Centers for Disease Control and Prevention, National Center for Injury Prevention and Control: https://www.cdc.gov/violenceprevention/pdf/NISVS-StateReportBook.pdf

but in a different direction. Could I become a part of this movement in my own way? No, that was far too scary a thought and just too much for me to take on.

Was it, though? What if I wrote about my sordid tale? A horrific crime was committed against me, yes. I could have buried it, forgotten it, and never spoken of it. Ever. But that was not—and still is not—me, and I actively chose *not* to do that. So, here I am. Speaking out on my own terms, like the many women before me, and I am here to help. Help spread awareness, help break the silence, help end the vicious cycle of sexual violence. If my story can help just one person to come forward, to heal, to confront their past, to know that everything is going to be okay, I have served my purpose.

This memoir goes there. It will catapult you out of your comfort zone and take you inside my jaded world. But I will also guide you out, give you hope, tell you a few things I have learned, and show you the other side. The other side is what has given me the courage to write this and hopefully will give you the courage to read it. In a way, this is my version of a self-help book. Don't worry; it's not one of those cheesy kinds you are thinking about. If you ever have or are currently going through something completely fucked up, with any luck this memoir will give you hope as you work your way through whatever it is you are dealing with. Because the other side does, indeed, exist.

Chapter 1
Here It Goes

L et me tell you all the ways to avoid getting raped.

Exactly. There are none. Sober or drunk, revealing clothes or sweats, makeup or none, it does not matter. It is never the victim's fault.

Here is my story.

Life is a funny thing. One day, it's there. You are living. And the next, it is gone. I was brushing my teeth that morning, as usual, and then I was lying half-naked in the front seat of a stranger's SUV with a knife to my neck. Not exactly how I thought that day would turn out. But let me back up.

I was twenty-two. Leading up to that age, I lived a pretty sweet life. If hashtags were a thing in 2008, I was definitely #livingthedream. I would never say I took my life for granted, and I would have liked to believe I "lived each day like it was my last," but I didn't. I mean, who does, really? Life gets in the way, and some days you go through the motions, do the routine; that worked for me. I was happy and feeling accomplished. I had just graduated from one of the top public universities in the country, and I was ready to tackle the next chapter of my life: moving away from my hometown to live in Washington, DC, working as an intern for a prestigious accounting firm amongst the city folk. I always thought I wanted to get out of Raleigh, North Carolina. It was the place I grew up, the place I knew best, the place most comfortable to me. However, I wanted to experience more.

My childhood was one of those you look back on and think to yourself, "Man, life was good." I was a pretty good kid. I obeyed my parents, did well in school, had nice friends, loved playing sports, and stayed out of trouble. My days were filled with creativity, freedom, fun, and laughter . . . well, for the most part. Raised by my mom, I never knew what it was like to have my mom and my dad living under the same roof. I did not come from a broken family; it was just a different type of family. My parents divorced when I was one, and I toggled back and forth between two houses every other weekend for much of my youth. My dad remarried when I was six and had three other kiddos: my twin half brothers and half sister (though I never refer to them as *half*—just a technicality). My mom also remarried and had my younger half brother. Basically, by the time I was eleven, I had this huge family with four sets of grandparents and extended clans. It was insane.

At the end of the day, it was my mom and I for the long haul, and I don't know what I would have done without her. She raised me to be independent, but also a team player. A leader, yet a follower when needed. A fighter for what I believed in, but also accepting of others. So, when I made that big move to the big city, I felt bigtime ready.

In the summer of 2008, I moved to Washington, DC, with my boyfriend (I'll refer to him as "Boyfriend") at the time, expecting it to be the summer of our lives. We were dating for a year and were completely enamored with each other. It was a *love at first sight* kind of thing the summer before. He came from Pennsylvania, I from North Carolina, and we met in the middle. So why not move in together, right? Wrong. Really, it could not have been a worse idea. We hunkered down in an 800-square-foot apartment with one bedroom and one bathroom in downtown Alexandria, Virginia. Coming from opposite parts of the East Coast into 800 square feet was a major adjustment, but what did we know? There were quite a few arguments, disagreements, worries about money, and overall bad attitudes toward one another. Nonetheless, we did have a few good moments in the first few weeks. That is, until June 29, 2008—a date etched in my mind for eternity. It was the day that changed my world as I knew it. Everything I thought I was, was gone. My dreams, shattered. My goals, no more. It was the day that set my story into motion.

Chapter 2
That Day

June 28, 2008. Three whole weeks into my big-city adventure. Just my average Saturday—I woke up, brushed my teeth, had some breakfast, and started making plans for the weekend. Boyfriend was invited to a cookout with a few of *his* friends and had made it disturbingly clear he planned to go solo. Not knowing anyone in the city, I blew up. "What do you mean I am not coming with you? What do you expect me to do?"

So there I was with no plans, by myself. I wasn't just going to sit there in the apartment. As it turned out, I had a distant cousin who lived in DC as well at the time, and my mom kept nudging me to reach out to her. Not having seen or talked to her since I was about ten years old, I was hesitant. My last memory of her was of us dancing at an aunt's wedding. We were literally ten. But on June 28, I really didn't have anything to lose, so I contacted her. We made plans to go out that night in the city, and I was nervous but relieved I actually had something to do.

"Cuz," as I shall call her, and I hit it off immediately. It was like we hadn't missed a beat in those twelve missing years. I thought to myself, *Okay, tonight may not be so bad.* We were with her boyfriend, who picked me up and drove us back to her apartment to pre-game. Pre-gaming: probably one of the best activities ever. Getting excited for the night, mapping out where to go, all while getting a decent buzz from the cranberry vodkas going down nice and easy.

That night, we headed to Adams Morgan, a place very different from my normal partying locales, and about eleven miles from Alexandria. It was like my college town on crack. Everything was bigger, more crowded, more expensive, but I loved it. Eventually switching to beer later in the evening, we danced, mingled, laughed, and then gorged on pizza. The fight earlier that day was put on hold, as I drunkenly and blissfully forgot about it as the night progressed. It really was the perfect night, or at least it started out that way. We headed back to my cousin's apartment at around 1 a.m., and I planned to spend the night there. However, like any girl who wants to make things better with her boyfriend, things changed.

I was a bit hazy during the hours from 1 to 3 a.m., but Boyfriend and I fought while I sat on the bathroom floor of Cuz's apartment. I know, keeping it classy. No clue what we argued about, but I'm sure it was a classic drunk fight—lots of yelling, cursing, crying, and blaming. Drunken fights are so pointless but seem so valid when they are happening. Crawling into bed after the showdown ended, I slowly started to drift to sleep. But then, one last phone call. It was Boyfriend saying I should come home. Well, duh. What girl wouldn't go home? So, there I was, at about 3:30 a.m., gearing up to head back home to Alexandria. My cousin graciously called me a cab after some serious convincing and assurance that I was making the right move. After all, I *had* to get home so that my relationship wouldn't be ruined forever.

I gave Cuz a tight hug and insisted she go back to sleep. She abided, and I decided to wait for this cab on the relatively well-lit sidewalk right outside her apartment. No cab. Called the company again. Still no cab. I sat down on the curb between two parked cars and was hidden from the street, contemplating how long I would wait to call again. Another few minutes passed, and then, finally, a dark-green SUV pulled up. It stopped exactly in between those two cars, right in the crevice of my view of the street. How oddly perfect.

Chapter 3
Shithead

╲·······╱

Thank God. The cab had arrived. The driver, a black man, rolled down the passenger-side window and hollered, "Hey! Where do you need to go?" I hopped off the curb in my jeans and cute navy-and-white tube top—they were the style that summer—and approached the SUV. Everything I wore that night was from Old Navy, my favorite, right down to the $2.50 flip-flops. Such a steal. I told him I needed to go to my apartment in Alexandria, and he replied, "Get in!" The cabbie said the back seat had too many things in it. I thought, *I don't want to sit on a bunch of crap, so the front seat it is.* I quickly glanced to the back of the SUV, and he was right.

Coming from my bubble college town in North Carolina, I was quite a novice cab rider, and at that moment I thought nothing of it. My only focus was getting home to Boyfriend, and this guy was going to take me there. Right after I shut the door and put my purse on the floor, I noticed he was on the phone with another customer. Or so I thought.

"Yeah, yeah, I'm going to Alexandria now, and could be there in about fifteen minutes," he said. *Sweet! That means only about ten minutes until I am home and finishing my amends,* I thought. I really had no clue where we were. After leaving Cuz's street, I vaguely remember a highway and some of those big green exit signs, but I was only ten minutes from home, like the cabbie said. *Good, good. Still no issues.*

A few minutes later, the phone call was ending, and, on the side of this highway, the car stopped. It was 4 a.m. with no other car in sight. The driver claimed he was lost and started to fidget with a few gadgets in the console, which was also filled with random shit. I knew I would probably not be of much help. After all, it was 2008, and I had a flip phone at best. No Google Maps, or Waze. If only I carried my Garmin with me in my purse. Or an actual old-school road map. Damn.

So we were lost, great. I still wasn't worried—*I mean, people get lost, right? But do cab drivers get lost? Hmmm, maybe I should be a little worried.* What felt like an eternity was probably only a minute, until he spoke.

Turning to me, he said, "I'm gonna need to see some tit before we go on." *Shit. Definitely not lost.* And now the worry started to kick in. The thoughts going through my mind were all over the place: *Did he really just say what I think he said? Who says the word "tit"? Am I dreaming? I am totally sober now, what a buzzkill. What is my next move? Can I get out of the car? I have no idea where the hell I am. How could I be so stupid to get in the front seat? Right, all the stuff in the back seat . . . I wonder what's back there, anyway.*

Then, boom. He was holding a knife. And he repeated himself, this time in a much louder, commanding voice. *Okay, he wins.* I pulled down my shirt, and out popped my "tit" that he so nicely referenced. He groped me, and I shuddered. From this point on, the cabbie, as I previously referred to him, would be known as "Shithead."

This was not good at all. Within milliseconds, he swiftly maneuvered over to my side of the car, landing on top of me. He pulled the seat lever down, unbuckled my seatbelt and put the knife to my neck. And he said, slightly louder than a whisper so I could hear him clearly, "If you scream, fight, or try to get away, I will kill you." So there I was, lifelessly lying there, envisioning my face on CNN. Headlines reading: "Caucasian Female in Early Twenties Found Dead on Some Highway in DC." Or maybe it wasn't DC. Could have been Virginia since he said I would be home in ten minutes. It had now been far longer than ten minutes. Boyfriend was definitely going to know something was up.

This could be it for me at just twenty-two years old. Had I accomplished everything I wanted to? How was my family going to find out? I was never really a religious person, but in my mind, I started talking to God. *Are you watching this, God? How is this going to end for me?* I said a quick prayer that I would live, and then I was catapulted back into what was happening in the front seat of this SUV. The knife was still on my neck, and I was frozen.

He was kissing my entire face, and his breath was like a never-emptied ashtray. I had to make a choice: *I either fight and risk dying, or I play into his sick little game and get out of this alive.* That whole "fight or flight" thing really did mean something. Except, I couldn't exactly do the "flight" part, seeing as how I was pinned down in a fucking car. And I didn't exactly want to fight because of the whole weapon situation. I thought, *Well, if he has a knife, perhaps he has a gun, too.* So, I decided to play the sick game. Fake it until you make it, right? Perhaps it would work. I kissed him back and put on my best show to make him think I was actually enjoying this rendezvous on the side of some thoroughfare. I was completely appalled, to the point where I thought I might get sick. I should have vomited in his mouth. He wouldn't have liked that too much.

Thankfully, I was able to keep my nauseated stomach at bay. On the other hand, Shithead was absolutely enjoying it. Moaning, even. Whispering, "Oh, yeah, you like that, don't you?" into my ear. *Why, yes, Shithead. I love this so much. Please continue.* Fucking asshole. I would have rather been gouging my eyes out. Literally anything sounded better than this current situation I was in. I hated him. Shithead kept on loving it. So much so that all of a sudden, he dropped the knife into the back of his car. *Thank God. My acting paid off; what a freaking idiot.* At any rate, he was no longer ready to slit my throat, and I was thankful for that. He continued with all the groping and moaning, and for a split second I thought I could grab that knife. I tried, but he wised up and shut me down with a firm "NO!" pinning my arms to the sides of the seat. *Okay, dude, you are still in control; calm down.* I whispered an apology and got back to my Oscar-worthy performance.

Thinking this crude asshole was almost done, I continued to comply. Sadly, I was wrong. He was not done, not even close. He told me to take off my pants. *My shirt off isn't enough? Come on, man.* I begged not to—I even offered to finish him off in different ways. He wasn't having it. I couldn't bear him pulling out another weapon. *What if he has a gun? Another knife?* So, off my pants came, and I knew what was happening next. His grimy hands quickly unbuttoned his own pants, and there in the dark with the faint light of a highway sign, I was lying naked with this stranger. The next several seconds lasted decades as he penetrated me. I didn't cry. I didn't make a sound. I didn't move. I may as well have been a statue, one that was knocked over on purpose—not broken yet, but about to crumble. I stared at the roof of his SUV. It was that velvety material, common on the ceilings of most vehicles. I remembered touching the velvet ceiling of my dad's car as a kid. It felt weird. If you swiped your finger fast on it, it burned. Hell if I know why I was thinking about that, at that exact moment, while Shithead raped me. But somehow it got me through it. How the hell was this happening?

He finished his business and then reached over me into his back seat of treasures and grabbed a towel. *Well, how nice of him to clean up; very thoughtful, what a gentleman.* He must have thought, *I just raped this girl. The least I could do is clean up my mess.* And with that, he pulled up his pants, buttoned them back up, and effortlessly returned to the driver's seat.

Minutes after we started driving again, I tried to reach for my phone. Shithead suspected that and made me give it to him. Of course, then my phone rang. I begged him to let me answer it. It was Boyfriend. Nobody else would be calling me at 4:30 a.m. I had started out ten minutes from home, and it was close to an hour later. Shithead conceded, gave me the phone, and I answered. "Hey, babe! Yeah, everything is fine, I'll be home soon!" *Click.* My acting had started going downhill; Boyfriend was frantic on the other end of the line, pleading me to tell him what was going on. Not wanting to let on that I was rattled in any way, I kept my composure. I listened to this sicko tell me he was sorry, and that he just couldn't help himself. *Give me a fucking break.* I muttered that it was "fine," desperately hoping my ride of horror was almost over. Then, to my surprise, minutes later we were in Alexandria. I finally recognized where we were, and I slyly guided him about a block from my apartment. No way was he going to see where I lived. The vehicle stopped, and I asked him his name. I thought since he apologized, maybe he was dumb enough to tell me his name. He didn't. I imagined he thought, *Smart move; she'll never know who I am.* Yeah, real smart, buddy.

Next thing I knew, it was time for me to exit the vehicle. This nightmare was over, and I was alive. I grabbed my purse, which he shockingly had no interest in, and got out of the car. I was escaping from this utter psycho of a man, and yet I took time to shut the car door. I had just been raped, was half naked, and really needed to take off running. However, I kindly shut the door to Shithead's car. This man, who just held a knife to my neck. This man, who said he was going to kill me. This man, who raped me. Who the fuck would take the time to shut his car door? Me. Must have been my upbringing. Raised to have good manners. Then I ran faster than I ever had in my life.

Chapter 4
That Morning

June 29, 2008. I was running down the street in Alexandria at about 4:45 a.m., screaming my head off, panicking, and trying to dial 9-1-1. *Dammit, I forgot to look at his license plate.* I must have been too focused on making sure his stupid car door was closed. I heard Boyfriend in the distance screaming my name, and I finally saw him. He was sprinting with a buddy of his, who apparently stayed at our apartment after the cookout. My pants were still half down, but I didn't care. Still running, we all came to a meeting point in the street. Boyfriend must have called the cops as well, because a police car suddenly appeared right next to us. I was in a state of shock and everything was a blur, but I vividly remember describing what had just occurred.

The police officer was indifferent to the information I provided, which didn't really piss me off until well after the fact. At any rate, he directed us to the sexual assault unit in downtown Washington, DC. We piled into Boyfriend's Jeep Wrangler, and down to the city we went. I would be lying if I said I remembered that ride. Overall, I remember being dirty and tainted but wanting to catch the son of a bitch who did this, so I calmly sat in the filth. I felt his stale cigarette breath emanating off me. It was most likely stinking up the car. Hopefully we put the windows down. All I knew was how determined I was to do everything I could to catch this guy, so I probably ignored it.

When we approached the station, the city was quiet and the sun was just coming up. It was so serene. The city sat there peacefully while I was just down the road lying with a monster. That peace was abruptly disrupted as the Jeep screeched to a halt in front of the building. I barged into the station shouting for some help. Two tall—one of them rather intimidating—African American detectives came to my aid. Boyfriend and his friend were with me, but we were soon separated, as I had to go in to give my statement—correction, loads of statements—alone. But I was in the mecca of police departments, right? I mean, this was Washington, DC, the capital of the United States. They had the best of the best here, right? Wrong. So, so wrong.

The detectives led me into a room that looked like a 1980s staged office. There was a plain oak table with four chairs, which we all sat around to let the "fun" begin. Initially, I was motivated to tell them what I had just been through. My love of Lifetime movies was really going to work in my favor. I had seen my fair share of plots where rape was involved, and I felt like I knew the steps in order to follow the necessary protocols:

No eating or drinking to preserve evidence

No shower or changing clothes, again to preserve evidence

Report the crime to the police

Go to the hospital for a rape kit

Seemed easy enough, right? As cheesy as Lifetime movies are, I was thankful for them in that motivational moment. However, as I sat there in my filthy clothes, covered in Shithead's DNA, no shower, no food, no water, no sleep, and feeling slightly hungover, my motivation started to slip away. One of the detectives started going through my phone. I was detailing exactly what happened to me, and rather than receiving any sympathy, I got questions about my text messages.

He inquired, "And who is this guy? Were you texting with him to try and get back at your boyfriend for making plans without you yesterday?" My initial thought was, *Are you fucking kidding me?* That was what he was focused on? He was referring to a friend from college who happened to ask how my summer was going, which I explained in a slightly irritated tone.

The other one then chimed in: "And how many drinks did you say you had? Are you sure you weren't just drunk?" Around and around we went for hours, me pleading my case and them not believing a word I said. I felt utterly defeated and exhausted. From what I knew about rape statistics, I suddenly understood why women weren't jumping at the immediate chance to report. To the detectives, I was just a white girl crying rape on a black man. I was too drunk to really remember what happened, and even worse, I couldn't tell them *where* it happened. But so what? Why wasn't I being taken seriously? Why weren't they trying to help me in any way they could?

Of course, they called the cab company my cousin had called hours earlier, and the company did not have record of my call. Great—another setback and another reason to call my bluff. I tried to explain how that couldn't be possible. I spoke directly to the company, and they informed me the cab was running late and it would be there to pick me up in five minutes. How could they not have record of my call? Left and right, I kept trying to defend myself, explain myself, say anything that would make my story credible. But all these detectives did was take notes and probe me with more questions. Then, because I couldn't recall where the rape took place, these assholes, Detective Dickhead #1 and #2, as I shall call them, decided it would be a good idea to put me in a cop car and drive around the DC/Northern Virginia area to try and jog my memory. Joy.

Still by myself, the detectives and I waltzed out of the police station and into a squad car. I was put in the front seat so I could really focus on the location of this supposed crime. I said, "You both realize I was sitting in the front seat of this guy's SUV when the attack occurred, and now you are making me sit in the front seat of your cop car, right?"

The more senior detective responded, "Ma'am, we need you to get in the car." Wow, what a way to revictimize the victim. But I complied, mainly because they were cops, and we are supposed to listen to and respect cops, right? So, I begrudgingly got into the car.

With Detective Dickhead #1 driving and #2 sitting directly behind me, I knew this was going to be torturous. At that point, it was now about

8 a.m. on Sunday, and there was still not much commotion around town. We drove all over the place. I kept recalling a green highway sign that said "Navy." Navy Yard, maybe? No, that wasn't it. We cruised highways, side roads, weaved in and out of Virginia and DC, and I point-blank couldn't remember. I begged myself to recall something, to recognize anything, but nothing. I finally admitted I didn't think I was going to pinpoint where the rape took place. I apologized profusely, as if it were my fault. For the second time that morning, Detective Dickhead #2 said, "I really think you were just drunk."

I couldn't even formulate words. If I could have, they would have come out something like, "Screw you, asshole. I told you what I know; take it or leave it. This happened to me, and it's on your hands now." In hindsight, I wish I had said *something*. But it was one of those classic moments in which you don't realize what you want to say until much later, and then it's too late. I continued to sit there and stare mindlessly out the window.

We were finally en route back to the station. I was relieved to know I would be out of that damn car soon. I really needed to get to the hospital so I could hand over all the evidence and get out of these disgusting clothes. As I thought about the next steps (from the Lifetime movies, of course), Detective Dickhead #1 all of a sudden pulled the car up onto a curb in the city and got out. We were at a friggin' Starbucks in downtown DC. Apparently, he needed a muffin and a latte to get him through the last stretch of our little car ride. He turned on the lights of the squad car, but not the siren, and #2 and I sat there waiting in silence. I must have been dreaming. But, no, out he came with his little white cup with the green goddess on it, and his paper bag also adorned with the green goddess, and got his ass back into the car. I peripherally watched him scarf down his muffin and sip casually on his coffee as we headed to the station. He was clearly very sympathetic to the fact that I could neither eat nor drink. Then again, maybe he thought I could since in his mind I was lying. What a necessary pit stop. I wanted to reach across the front seat and punch him.

When we arrived back at the sexual assault unit, Boyfriend and his friend were sitting outside. Relieved to see them both, I leapt out of the car immediately to end the horrendous tour around the District. We wrapped things up on the unit's front steps. Basically, the detectives said something to the effect of, "We will let you know if we come across anything. We wouldn't recommend calling your mom or anything, as this will all blow over and be fine. Best of luck."

WHAT? Not call my mom? With complete offense to both of you degenerates, you don't know my mother and our relationship, and I can call whomever the hell I want. No, this is not going to just blow over and go away. And no, I am not fine. You will be hearing from me because I am not going away, so I hope you are both ready because you just met your worst nightmare.

Of course, none of these words actually came out of my mouth. This was another one of those classic moments of kicking myself, well after the fact, for not speaking my mind. But at least I am saying them now. As I got in the car after a weary five hours, I decided to call my mom.

With my stomach in my throat, I dialed. It seemed like an hour went by before she answered. How was I going to relay this information? Just come out with it? Have some small talk before? I wasn't a parent at the time, but I knew this was going to be the worst call of her life.

"Hey, Gird!" she said happily. (One of her many nicknames for me, Girdie, was adapted from *girlie*.)

"Hey, Mom, I have to tell you something. Please know that I am okay now."

Radio silence for a few seconds, then she replied, "Oh, my God, what's wrong?" I proceeded to recount the events of the wee morning hours. Her response was a mixture of panic, worry, and sadness as she called out, "I'm coming to you right now." She happened to be at our mountain cabin in Boone, North Carolina, with my younger brother for a quick getaway, which meant she was about four hours further from DC than if she'd been home in Raleigh. That was my mom. She was going to formulate a plan and get to me as soon as she could, whatever it took.

She then quickly said, "Okay, okay, I'm leaving immediately. I'm going to get your brother back to Raleigh and then hit the road to DC."

I assured her I was physically all right and had just left the police station. Boyfriend called his parents right after everything happened at around 5 a.m., so they were already on their way from Philadelphia to DC. And so off we went to our next stop, the Howard University Hospital.

Chapter 5
That Afternoon

Imagine one of those hospital shows like *Grey's Anatomy*, or a major throwback, *ER*, where a woman stumbles through the front doors of the establishment, discombobulated, looking disheveled, exhausted, and not really having a clue about what to do or where to go. That was me. My admittance into the hospital was a bit of a blur. Boyfriend handled a lot of it. The SANE (sexual assault nurse examiner) nurse on-call was paged, but she was two hours from getting to the hospital. Two hours. I mean, I get that she was on-call, but damn! What was another two hours, though, when it had been a hundred already (or so it seemed)? I was going to stay dirty, contaminated, starved, thirsty, overly tired, but full of adrenaline. Hey, at least I was no longer with the spawns of Satan at the police station.

We were led to a small room with a few benches and bare walls. It had doors, so thankfully I didn't have to sit among the emergency room folk in the public waiting room. There we would wait until I was called in for my rape kit examination. Within a few minutes, Boyfriend's parents arrived. I was so relieved to see familiar faces and yet embarrassed that they were seeing me in this fashion. Boyfriend's parents weren't thrilled we were living together in DC, and now this. Not to my surprise, they were wonderful, nonjudgmental, and overly willing to fill in as my loving parents until my own arrived. They didn't pry for any information that I wasn't willing to share. I sat there on that bench, partly in silence, partly in conversation. I wasn't crying. I hadn't really cried yet. Why wasn't I crying? I remember saying I felt like I was having an out-of-body experience and telling the story of a ghost person sitting on the bench next to me. This didn't *actually* happen to me, did it? Disassociation actually allowed me to speak about what happened pretty freely.

A few more minutes elapsed, and a victim advocate from the hospital came into our tiny waiting room. She sat across from me and explained that she was there to help me with whatever I needed. She would sit with me, talk with me, and go into the exam room with me. All very helpful things, yes, but she couldn't give me a shower, give me food, give me something to drink, airlift the SANE nurse to me so this godforsaken day could come to an end. But it was a nice gesture, and it was comforting to have another person to sit with.

Tick, tock, tick, tock. I had a horrid taste in my overly dry mouth—a mixture of the previous night's alcohol and cigarette ash. What I wouldn't do for a toothbrush. My head was pounding, and my eyelids felt like cinder blocks, but every time I tried to close my eyes, the cinder blocks disappeared, and my eyelids flew back open. The minutes dragged along until finally I was called to begin my rape kit exam. Little did I know what this process entailed.

The advocate led me out of our private waiting area into the exam room. The room was bright. There was a large table for me to lie on and an ungodly number of evidence bags sitting next to it. The nurse explained what was going to happen—lots of picking, swabbing, collecting. I was ready for this. This man was coming off me and going straight into bags. Thank God. And so it began.

The nurse inspected every part of my body with a fine-toothed comb, pulling hairs off with tweezers, swabbing my cheek with Q-tips, and lifting DNA from my lips and face. With each new body part, I removed that piece of clothing and into a bag it went. At one point, I looked down at my chest, and a coarse, curly, black hair was sticking out of my tube top. I almost gagged and quickly had the nurse grab it before it fell off me into oblivion. She inspected my arms, where bruises had begun forming.

I flashed back for a minute. *Where did those bruises come from? Ah yes, right after I tried to reach for the knife, Shithead tightened his grip on my arms. Got it. Okay, back to reality now.* Tube top off, then bra, after which I was able to put on some *clean* clothes that Boyfriend brought from home, and then onto my lower half.

The lower body examination took the longest. As I removed my jeans, I shuddered thinking what they would find down there. Semen, evidence of tearing, some bleeding, and overall trauma to my vaginal region. I grew angry in that moment. This prick had violated me in the worst way possible. What was Shithead doing that afternoon while I lay here getting poked and prodded? Did he go right home? Did he even have a home to go to? Maybe he went to breakfast. He had quite an action-packed night. All that I knew of him was going into bags, and I was one step closer to showering him off.

After three hours of examining, the nurse and police had everything they could get from my body. I then learned I would never get my clothes back. Dammit. Those were the most comfortable Old Navy jeans I owned. And it was the best Victoria's Secret strapless bra! It didn't create back fat and didn't show through shirts from the front. But, hey, the hospital was giving me a whole $100 to get new clothes. What a treat. Thanks to my rapist, I could go on a little shopping spree.

I finally sat up on the cold table, thinking I was good to go, but no, not yet. It was now time for the cocktail of medications. To avoid pregnancy, syphilis, gonorrhea, crabs, scabies, herpes, and any other STD you could think of, I had to ingest about thirteen pills on an empty stomach. The nurse said, "I know this is not ideal, but you have to keep these meds down or else you will have to take them again." I hadn't even considered I could contract a disease from rape. I willingly took everything and told myself not to vomit.

Suddenly a terrifying thought popped into my head that made my heart fall into my stomach. I blurted out to the nurse, "So what about HIV?"

The nurse looked at me solemnly and began explaining that HIV was a bit of a different beast. I think I blacked out for a minute. *What if this fucking asshole gave me HIV?* The nurse said HIV is something that could show up well after the fact. *Oh, okay, great.*

I asked, "Like how long after the fact?"

Nurse replied, "A year."

An ENTIRE YEAR? Oh, dear God, you have got to be kidding me. I sat there and put my heavy head in my hands and stayed that way for a few minutes. They would run blood work that day, but I would have to get my blood drawn every three months for the next year. Then wait and see. *Wait and see. And then what?* Good Lord, if this wasn't already bad enough.

Another lovely thought entered my brain about the pregnancy aspect, which also scared me shitless. There was no way in hell I could keep a rapist's baby. Not to get political, as I absolutely despise discussing anything to do with politics, but I would not be able to keep it. Judge away, but I couldn't do it. At that point, in my mind, I was a pregnant rape victim with HIV. I had the tendency to snowball to the worst-case scenario, but could you blame me?

Moments later, another nurse brought me the most appetizing plate of hospital food I had ever seen. I inhaled a delicious turkey sandwich and Jell-O. What more could a girl want? Unfortunately, the meds hit my stomach before the food did, and next thing I knew, I was pacing up and down the hospital hallway trying not to get sick.

I felt faint, nauseated, and broken. I had now been awake for more than twenty-four hours. *Come on, self, you got this. You've come this far and are in the home stretch now.* I was in my clean pajamas; granted, my body wasn't clean, but it was a step in the right direction. I had eaten food, and apparently I was preventing all sorts of diseases from developing inside me. More pacing up and down the hallway, repeatedly telling myself, *Keep those meds down and you're golden.* After about an hour, I had done it. Go me! Discharge was coming, and I would finally, FINALLY, get to go home and think about ending this terrible day.

Chapter 6
That Night

My apartment. Everything was different now. I stood there, in the place that about fourteen hours earlier I avoided like the measles so Shithead wouldn't know where I lived. And before that, I was in the same apartment getting ready to go out. Thirty-some-odd hours later, and I was a different person in that same apartment. What the hell happened? I was just supposed to be going out with a cousin I met once when I was ten. Now, I had a rape, an interrogation, and one hell of a hospital visit under my belt. Seriously, though, what the hell happened?

By the time I got home, my mom had finally arrived after her trek across the state of North Carolina and up to Northern Virginia. My stepdad, who was on business in New York, flew in. And Boyfriend's parents were there. Six people in a one-bedroom, one-bathroom apartment, and I could have had more. These people would keep me safe, not let me out of their sight, not let anything else bad happen to me. The only things on my mind were a shower and more food. The filth on my body had been there long enough. As I stood in our closet taking off my shirt, Boyfriend came in and immediately dropped to his knees sobbing. The horror, guilt, anger, and sadness flooded him, and he couldn't speak. Neither could I. Everything was different now. I just stood there—couldn't cry, didn't talk. I was numb and really, really dirty. I motioned Boyfriend out of the closet so I could get in the long-awaited shower.

Imagine you're an astronaut who has been away from Earth for ages, and the only thing you want to do when you get there is take a shower. That was me. It was as if water were hitting my body for the first time, even though I had stood in that shower the day before. Everything was different now. The water worked its way over my broken body. I soon realized tears were mixed in with the water. Finally. It felt good to cry. It didn't last long, but it was a small release.

I may have broken the record for the longest shower that night. I kept washing and washing, hoping to feel clean, but I didn't. More scrubbing—washcloth, loofa, my hands. There wasn't enough soap in the world to convince my brain that Shithead was gone. I kept feeling his breath, his tongue, his hands, the weight of his body over mine. I tried to keep my eyes open while the water fell on my face for the fear that once I closed them, there he would be. This shower that I hoped would be epic was a complete letdown. I had done everything I was supposed to do given the day I just had: stayed alive, reported the crime, got myself treated at the hospital, made it home. Why couldn't I do something I wanted to do? Shithead was still there: in my mind, in the shower, in my apartment. He was everywhere, and everything was different now.

I decided it was time for the shower to end. What next? I honestly didn't know. *Try to go to sleep, I suppose.* And it hit me how absolutely exhausted I was. Stepping out of the shower, my body felt like a ton of bricks. I caught a glimpse of myself naked in the mirror. Yikes, what a scary sight. The light arm bruises from Shithead's grip were getting darker, and my otherwise pale skin looked worn, like it had been run over by a bus. I lifted my head to look at my neck and instantly experienced a horrific flashback to the knife. It was a long blade—pretty sharp, I would imagine. I remembered the metal ever so slightly grazing my skin. Chills coursed down my spine. Now that I thought about it for a minute, I was not completely sure if it was a pocketknife or much larger one. It definitely wasn't a butter knife. It came out of nowhere, but thankfully didn't leave a mark, only a disturbing memory. That bastard.

I heard my mom call for me and ask if I was all right. The answer was no. But I didn't say that. I said I was almost done. So, I guess I didn't really answer her question. Oh well.

Everything was different now.

Putting on my second pair of pajamas, this time on a physically clean body, I emerged from the bathroom to join the other five people in my apartment. Boyfriend's mom had made me scrambled eggs, per my request. After all, that was the next meal I was supposed to eat, as I had missed breakfast that morning. (But man am I glad Detective Dickhead #1 didn't. Asshole.) Scrambled eggs are delicious. A true staple at breakfast, and one of the few foods I am actually good at making. It was the first food that popped in my head, so I went with it.

After my 9 p.m. breakfast, I crawled into bed. It dawned on me that I never called my cousin to tell her what happened. How could I tell her, though? I was picked up right outside her apartment, which I guess one could argue was the very reason I should tell her. But I had just met her, and what if she told people in our family? No, I couldn't tell her. Maybe later.

My mom slept with me, while everyone else was on the couch and blow-up air mattresses, and within earshot. I needed everyone close by. If we could have all fit in one bed, that would have been nice. Finally, it was time to sleep. I closed my eyes. *Fuck, Shithead again.* His disgusting face and whispers and curly short hair and gross fingernails filled the darkness behind my eyelids. *Come on, you asshole; feel free to go away anytime now.* But he didn't. He was there to stay, for a very, very long time.

Chapter 7
The Next Day

⌒・・・・・・⌒

I got maybe an hour of actual sleep, but fortunately I felt more rested than the day before. It was a Monday, and I was definitely not making it to the office for my internship. Interns didn't get any vacation time and only received approved days off for rare instances. Surely this would classify as an excused absence, right?

Anxiety ridden over the possibility this would affect a full-time job offer, my mom decided to call the intern human resources manager, a woman I had met maybe twice. The call lasted about ten minutes, and when my mom got off the phone, she assured me everything was more than okay. The accounting firm was allowing me to take as much time as I needed, with absolutely no penalty. HR would handle all communications to my teams and fellow interns. To say I was relieved was an understatement. What an amazing HR manager and, furthermore, an amazing company.

The rest of that Monday was weird. I didn't know what to do, or if I should be doing anything at all. I couldn't sleep. Didn't want to go anywhere. Didn't want to see anyone other than those already in my apartment. But I did want something, and that something was penuche fudge. If you've never had penuche fudge in your life, you are seriously missing out. This fudge was a longtime family tradition on my mom's side. My grandmother made it when I was a little girl, and I became an instant addict. It's the epitome of comfort food for me. I looked at my mom with a small smirk on my face and said, "Mom. I know what I need. FUDGE!"

She instantly hopped up and replied, "I'll go to the store now to get the stuff." The "stuff" in penuche fudge is basically brown sugar, milk, vanilla, butter, and some more butter—clearly exceptionally low in fat. My mom returned from the store in record time and started the hour-long fudge-making process. I spent the rest of the day sneaking spoon dips into the boiling mixture and then gorging on the entire pan of penuche. It instantly made me feel better and provided me with a brief mental break from the rape aftermath. *Brief* being the key word.

Chapter 8
Beads

Ever have those moments in life when you are so overwhelmed you just need to escape? That was me. But I didn't know that escaping was what I needed. Thankfully, my mom did. My life felt like scattered beads all over the floor from a broken clasp on a necklace, moving in different directions, going nowhere good: some going under the dresser, never to be found again, and some to be stepped on and make indentions in your feet. Some you pick up right away, nervously trying to put the necklace back together. And some you just stop looking for but find many years later. I operated like a broken puppet in my scattered-bead life. I not only needed to be put back together, but I needed to be moved and told what to do. Me, make a decision? Forget it. My mom would suggest all my activities from eating to showering to sleeping, and I willingly followed because I couldn't think past that moment. After a few days of hibernating and eating fudge in my apartment, my mom decided to take me away from Alexandria to our cabin in Boone. I was an easy sell. It sounded great.

My escape from the chaos began with several hours in the car. To some, it may sound painfully boring. However, for me, it was heaven. I opted to sit in the back seat of my mom's SUV so I could stretch out and have some space. After all, the past two rides I experienced were in a cop car and Shithead's SUV, both in the *front* seat. I spent those heavenly hours staring out the window, admiring nature. I had never seen highway flowers so beautiful. There were so many colors—orange, yellow, purple.

Who planted those? Or were they wild? I had never noticed or cared about that before.

My mom did a verbal check-in with me every so often to make sure I was okay. Occasionally, she reached her hand around the back of her seat to physically make sure I was there. She knew I was, but it comforted her to actually make contact. As we neared Boone, she suggested making a pit stop at Michaels, the craft store. Jackpot!

I love a good craft. Scrapbooks and rows of stickers get my creative juices flowing. Don't get me started on all the different kinds of pens in every color, all individually organized in their black canisters. You can't just buy one, because then you don't see *all* the colors together, which is the best part. You have to get them all. So, yeah, I'm a craft junkie. As we entered Michaels, my mom said I could literally get anything in the store I wanted. *Anything? I can buy all the pens I want?* I was giddy. With all of Michaels at my disposal, you'd think I had just won the lottery.

I started wandering the aisles, in amazement of all the craft possibilities. I had been in Michaels countless times prior to this instance, but this time was far different. I had a newfound appreciation for everything—every piece of paper, every photo box, every picture frame. I loved it all. I loved it because I was still alive to see it. I loved it because I had the time to admire it. I loved it because it made me feel safe. Crafts were an escape for me. Using my imagination to create something delicate and pretty brought me comfort. Crafting was therapeutic and an outlet. Through these thoughts, I stumbled upon the prize. I suddenly knew what I would get: All. The. Beads.

The bead aisle at Michaels was magnificent. There were bags of beads, bins of individual beads, bead books, bead tutorials, bead everything. I went to town, and started loading my cart. Countless beads, jewelry supplies, and books quickly found their way into my possession. I got hooks, chains, pliers—I could have started my own bead boutique. I patiently gazed at each item as the cashier rang it up and placed it in a bag. The grand total: $400! And my mom bought it all. These weren't just beads, after all. They were my world—my new world after my old world had gone to shit. I always viewed my mom as a saint, but that day, she was an extra special saint. She later told me she didn't really know what else to do, but she knew Michaels would do something good and healthy for me, and she was right.

For the next two weeks in the mountains, I played with these beads every single day. Earrings, necklaces, bracelets, key chains—you name it, I made it. These beads were like the pieces of jewelry you try and substitute for the necklace that just scattered all over the floor. I wasn't going to "find" or "clean up" those beads anytime soon. So, these beads were my temporary survival. And I was proud of myself. Each day, I enjoyed mini accomplishments that felt like I was moving mountains. I was doing it by myself in our cabin loft—with my mom downstairs, of course, but *I* was doing it. These beads gave me purpose. Laying out my gray-felted jewelry tray with all its compartments for the various clasps and hooks was like setting up my office for the day. Mindless TV played in the background— Lifetime movies on repeat—and my mom would deliver food to me from the kitchen downstairs. Each time she came up, she would gently pat my shoulder, providing her with peace of mind that I was physically with her. Some days I would talk to Boyfriend. Some days I wouldn't. He was still in DC, working, going out with friends, trying to be normal. What the hell was normal? My normal revolved around what show-stopping piece of jewelry I would make next.

One small silver lining: I was not pregnant. My period came, and I've never been so happy to see that sucker. Oh, and I didn't have HIV, at least not yet. My mom called the hotline to get my results. Nothing like a mother-daughter bonding moment, sitting and waiting for HIV results. We waited and waited, and I almost shit myself. Negative. Thank the Lord. Moving on.

At night, my mom slept in the same bed with me to assure me the nightmares weren't reality. I would sit straight up in bed after gasping back into life, and she softly stroked my arm until I went back to sleep. I needed my beads in the daytime. I hated nights. No beads. No happy thoughts. This was the cycle for two weeks straight: beads by day, nightmares and arm stroking by night—happy, sad, happy, sad. When those two weeks ended, I knew I *needed* to get back to my internship and finish what I started in DC. I *needed* a sense of normalcy beyond the beads. So what better way to gain that than to thrust myself back into my old life as best I could?

I never really looked at my beads again. In fact, they are still in a bag up on a shelf in my closet. Looking back, I should have stuck with the beads because the days and years ahead were going to be the hardest of my life, and I had no idea what I was in for.

Chapter 9
Back to Reality

Eminem couldn't have said it better. His lyrics may as well have been written in anticipation of my 2008 existence. My reality had no gravity. I floated through each day, going through the motions and praying that my underlying secret wouldn't expose itself. Returning to my internship, everyone wanted to know why I was gone. "Interns aren't allowed to take vacation, so why did she get one?" was one of the rumblings I heard. I made up some jackass story about a family emergency, something to do with medical issues. I was always shaky at first when telling my fake reason, but I got really good at it. *Hey, this isn't so bad.* The conviction in my voice became so effective I even started to believe I was gone for a family emergency.

Unfortunately, the terrifying thoughts usually came flying back into my brain like daggers, quickly reminding me that I definitely wasn't gone for a family emergency. *Damn.* I carried on, waiting for my absence to become old news, which it did relatively quickly, thank God. I tried to get back to normal as best as possible. Hell, I even went on the end-of-internship trip to Disney World for all interns who received a full-time offer. A month after my attack, I traveled to "the Happiest Place on Earth"—how ironic.

I was very strategic in building my support system. I tried to choose people I knew wouldn't judge me, those I wouldn't have to take care of because they were so devastated by what happened to me. Most listeners handled the news as I would have—supportive, shocked, devastated for me, and so on. Unfortunately, some mistakes were made along the way in this selection process. At one point, I found myself apologizing for the listener becoming so upset. What the fuck? Why was I apologizing? I didn't do anything wrong. This was particularly hard for me because it made me even more vulnerable and closed off than I already was. Some days, I wanted to scream from the rooftops that I was raped. But then I risked exposure, and everyone would know my deep, dark secret. Other days, I just wanted to go back to normal, like nothing ever happened— but I wasn't normal, and so much had happened. I wanted everyone to know, and then I didn't.

Ultimately, I decided the best course of action was for me to hold off from shouting my truth from the rooftops. However, I did choose my select few. I made sure I had at least one person "in the know" in each area of my life: work, family, and friend circle. These "knowers," as I referred to them, allowed me to create my ultimate secret-keeping weapon: my new identity.

Chapter 10
The Face

B ecause there were so many people who didn't know about my secret, I mastered an alter ego, which I appropriately named "Face." Face was amazing. Everything was back to normal in my Face world. I was happy, fun, carefree, and didn't worry about my secret at all. One person for whom I put on the Face persona was my dad. To this day, I can't think of a good reason as to why I never immediately told him about the rape. We had a fine relationship at that point in my life, but I never got around to it. Historically, my mom was my go-to for everything happy, sad, mad, whatever I felt. I suppose subconsciously I stuck to what I knew. It seemed easier to put Face on than to divulge, and I didn't know how to broach the subject with him. As with anything you do over and over, Face became second nature, almost easy for me to conceal my truths.

In my efforts to bury and suppress the darkness of prior weeks, I went through the motions of life. I told myself everything was good. I went to my internship every day. I grocery shopped, brought my clothes to the dry cleaners, attempted adult conversations, showered, and tried carrying on business as usual. But it wasn't usual; in fact, it was the most unusual I had ever been in my twenty-two years of life. I needed to do business as usual because if I didn't, I would shatter into a million pieces.

I didn't realize how exhausting it was keeping up my type A personality, post-rape. I was crumbling inside but did not always let myself acknowledge it. My attacker was still out and about in the world, living freely, and here I was hiding behind Face. I was living in this shell of my former self, trying desperately to get back to that person, but she did not exist anymore. I felt lost. I longed for control, consistency, familiarity, and protection from the dangers of the world. The truth of the matter was I had none of those. Or at least I didn't feel like I did. Regardless of how good Face was, and it was superb, it was completely external. Face became an ironclad barrier to my inside world. Suppression felt like the best coping mechanism at the time. After all, I needed to focus on my relationship with the guy I loved deeply. But he was slipping away, and I knew it.

Chapter 11
The End

❦ • • • • • ❧

Face could not mask my crashing and burning relationship. It was a slow crash and burn, but a crash and burn nonetheless. Things weren't great even before the rape. I would never place the blame for that evening on anyone other than Shithead, but Boyfriend and I were apart that evening for a reason. Things weren't great before, and they definitely were not great after. Looking back, we were not strong enough to weather the aftermath post-rape, and I don't know that many couples would have been at twenty-one and twenty-two years old. However, I wanted to think we could make it.

We didn't have sex, for the obvious reasons that I was not in a place to do so, but we didn't even really touch. We barely spoke, and we lived in 800 square feet of space. What was supposed to be a cozy, loving environment became cold and lonely. It's human nature to crave what we don't have. The more needy I became, the more Boyfriend pulled away. The more he pulled away, the more desperate I became. All of my attention-seeking tactics failed. I tried excessively coughing to get a glance in my direction. Didn't work. I tried asking stupid questions that I already knew the answer to. Received one-word answers. I tried asking for him to bring me something, like a glass of water. He'd reply that he was preoccupied, and it'd be quicker if I got it myself. Thus, in a very short period, I became this person I never wanted to be. I was a rape victim, and now I was the classic needy girlfriend. Gross.

One of my larger gestures to rekindle the romance seemed like the perfect idea at the time. Boyfriend was out of town for work, and he was coming home that Saturday evening. I was so excited, giddy even, because I was going to surprise him at the airport. What a way to kick things back into gear! Or so I thought.

A girlfriend and I got drinks beforehand at this DC bar, the Froggy Bottom—a play on the District neighborhood called Foggy Bottom. It was a fun little spot where the pitchers of beer were flowing. Drinking was becoming one of my favorite hobbies, and I did not disappoint that evening. I needed several drinks in order to go to the airport because, deep down, I knew Boyfriend and I weren't going to make it. However, I was still going to give it my all, and this particular attempt happened to involve several beers.

My excitement and anticipation grew by the minute. Finally, it was time to go surprise Boyfriend! I parted ways with my girlfriend and hopped on the metro en route to Reagan National Airport, a.k.a. "the Ronald," as I drunkenly named it. I told strangers on the metro about my plans to surprise Boyfriend at the Ronald—everyone loved it, or at least I thought they did. I mean, people probably do airport surprises all the time, but I was not only doing an airport surprise, I was going to save my relationship! Rachael to the rescue at the Ronald! It was the perfect plan and had to work, right?

As the metro crawled closer and closer, I thought about those movie scenes at the airport where the guy and girl run toward each other, jump into one another's arms, and hug and kiss and fireworks explode. That was totally going to be us. Holy shit, I could not have been more wrong.

I saw Boyfriend, and I started running toward him. He looked at me and coldly said, "What are you doing here?" Wow, not exactly the reception I was hoping for. There was no hug, no kiss, and definitely no fireworks. Completely taken aback, I mumbled something about wanting to surprise him, which obviously meant nothing. He walked briskly past me, clearly pissed that I showed up in the first place. He later claimed he was embarrassed at how drunk I was in front of his fellow interns he flew home with. Bullshit. He flat out didn't want to see me, and that was the devastating reality. So now I was the rape victim and the needy girlfriend whose boyfriend didn't need her back.

What little I had left to give was gone. We were done, the end, that was it. That night and the days that followed, I just cried. It all hit me like a million sandbags. The summer was over, my relationship was over, my time in DC was over, and my life as I knew it was over. We didn't go through the formality of a break-up while still in DC; we did that after moving back to our respective college towns—Boyfriend to start his senior year, and me to embark to Chapel Hill for the blur that was grad school.

Chapter 12
The Blur

Grad school was the longest and shortest and blurriest year of my life. Over the summer of hell, I contemplated withdrawing from my master of accounting program. I had been through too much, and I needed time to put some semblance of a life back together. But what did that actually entail? Putting my life back together—let's paint that picture.

I would have to move back home with my mom because I had no money. I would see some friends occasionally, maybe. They were all working and making something of themselves, though, so maybe not. Maybe I'd get a job. Doing what? I had a full-time offer from the accounting firm where I interned, but it would mean nothing if I didn't go to grad school. I could sleep in every day and rely on my mom to take care of me while I wallowed in sadness and misery about being a rape victim. I could throw myself a big pity party every day and remind myself that I was a rape victim while the world continued spinning around me. "Sounds fun," said no one ever. So, I decided I would keep my original plan and go to grad school. After all, I still had Face, and Face never disappointed.

Even though I moved back to the exact same town I lived in just a few months prior, it all felt different. The last time I was there, I was happy. I had just graduated, I was in a fantastic relationship, and I was moving to the big city. But now, my life was all over the place. I was back not because I wanted to be but by default, in a way, because I didn't want the alternative: self-pitying at home. Luckily for me, it was time for another round of HIV testing. Something you never think you'll have to do in your life: find a lab to get blood drawn to see if a rapist gave you HIV. I went, did the blood work, and waited for however many days until my results were in. My mom called again, because I just couldn't bear to hear it. Negative for round two. Thank the Lord.

My once straight and narrow plans for the future were now a big ball of mush. The first few weeks of school were, well, I can't really remember, to tell you the truth. I went to class, attempted to not completely fail, and then I would go back to my apartment and work on this monstrosity of a scrapbook from when I studied abroad a year earlier. The scrapbook was my new form of beads—something I could control and immerse myself in to forget about the chaos surrounding me. I would sit there and meticulously cut faux stones out of black and gray construction paper to create the illusion of a cobblestone road, which I then carefully glued diagonally across a piece of scrapbook paper, followed by photos that were truly taken on a cobblestone road. I got into it, to say the least. It worked for a little while, until everything got even shittier when my relationship officially ended.

The person I thought would be my husband and I ended our relationship over the phone. THE PHONE. Granted, there were several states between us, but it really should have ended in person. It was bound to happen, and when it finally did, I was the one to pull the trigger. Then came the regret, devastation, nausea, and numbness over the following days, all while still trying to make it to class. I slept in the same bed with my roommate, who was a knower and super supportive, the first few nights after the phone breakup. I couldn't handle physically being alone, and she would come get me after hearing the sobs through her bedroom wall.

I called my mom, sobbing. It was definitely an "I'll put on the fudge" moment—my mom coined the phrase to create a sliver of light in crisis situations. Thankfully, she only lived about forty-five minutes away from my college, so I had easy access to said fudge. I deactivated and reactivated my social media account about eighty-three times in two days—one of those attention-seeking tactics I became so keen on. That, of course, accomplished nothing. Boyfriend didn't try to contact me at all. He was done. Free. Relieved. He was no longer the boyfriend of a rape victim. It must have been nice to be done with that burden.

Years later, I did discover the breakup hit him hard. He sobbed all night and stayed away from relationships for a while. Not that it mattered, but it would have been nice to hear that information much sooner; in my mind, he was living his best life, partying with girls, and so on. In reality, though, not much would have helped me at that point. I was essentially a lost cause struggling to maintain Face. Most people continued to fall for my act, but one person didn't.

One random day after class, my business law professor asked to see me in her office. *Hmmm, what did I do? Am I failing? Did she catch me doing a crossword when I should have been listening to her discuss business combinations?* I walked into her office, sat down, and she immediately said, "Okay, what is going on with you?"

Here was the background on this professor: I aced her undergrad law class the semester before. You know, when my life was happy and on that stringent path to success. She was one tough cookie, and she grew to become one of my favorites. Lucky for me, she also taught tax law in my graduate program. Face didn't fool her. Damn lawyers. At any rate, I tried to evade the truth initially by responding with a "What do you mean? I'm fine!" Yeah, that didn't work.

So, I ended up giving her the CliffsNotes version of my attack, my breakup, my wavering decision to stick with grad school, and the fact that I had no idea how I was going to make it. The CliffsNotes version turned into word vomit. She was the first person who called my bluff, who wasn't a knower, and I utterly crumbled. My professor's usual stoic persona cracked a little. She stayed true to her lawyer and professor role, *but* she looked me straight in the eye and told me I could do this. She said she was deeply sorry for everything I went through, and I felt her sincerity. However, she believed in me and knew the old me, and knew I could get through this program.

I don't think she realized quite how pivotal she was in my journey. Don't get me wrong, I still went down a dark and spiraling tunnel, but I at least saw a glimmer of hope of finishing what I had started. The glimmer, tiny as it was, gave me the strength to say, "To hell with it," and do something WAY out of my element.

Chapter 13
Live Laugh Love

I know, I know. *Live Laugh Love* is super cliché, but I really love this little saying that can be found on anything from a small, inspirational notebook to a city billboard. I always have. I never fully *lived* by it, though. I was stuck on that whole straight and narrow thing, remember? I lived, for sure, but within a ridiculous amount of control and order. I laughed and relaxed when my to-do list was done. I loved, but not if that love was going to disrupt my organized world. I was completely content with this way of living. I concealed my neuroses to an extent and could definitely let loose, but I loved order.

When the rape happened, order went out the window. My world shifted, and I found myself delving into the meaning of this saying. What would happen if I did something out of order, something that never would have crossed my mind, and truly *lived* outside my cookie-cutter lifestyle? Like . . . get a tattoo.

Yes, I was going to get a tattoo. This type A accounting guru was going to walk into one of those grungy tattoo parlors and get inked by a guy whose body you could barely see behind all of *his* tattoos. This idea gave me the biggest surge of excitement I had experienced in months. I set out with my design ideas and landed on a gold mine: the female—Venus—symbol, with the circle and the cross, only the circle would spell out my beloved phrase, *Live Laugh Love*. It was perfect. Talk about empowerment. I was about to rock the epitome of strength, even though

I wasn't exactly feeling strong. Fake it till you make it, right? What better way to do that than to have a permanent reminder on your body?

My best friend in the universe (Bestie, as I shall call her) ventured to the tattoo parlor with me. What a sight: two Caucasian, blonde females with no tattoos walking into a place where there was nothing but tattoos. We definitely got some looks, but the atmosphere gave me a rush. The fact that I didn't fit in gave me comfort in my own rebellious way. *Take that, rapist.* Shithead disrupted my order, so I was making the best of it. The tattoo artist drew my vision perfectly, all in black ink. He put the design onto a piece of wax paper and placed it where I wanted it. Pressing down, the ink transferred to my skin so he would have his outline. Within five minutes, which felt like five hours, there it was on my right shoulder blade. Dripping in sweat, I came off the chair with the understanding that I now had to do a better job of living, laughing, and loving because it was now permanently *on me.* It didn't exactly do the trick until years later, but it was a tiny step in the right direction.

Chapter 14
The Old Becomes the New (Again)

About six months after the attack, three or so months after my breakup with Boyfriend, I was at my favorite place, the bar, when I got a phone call. It was Bestie, who was also in Chapel Hill, and she said, "You're never going to guess who I just ran into."

Oh, dear God, it could be anyone. "Who?" I responded with alcohol-induced angst.

"D Brooks!" she exclaimed. *Ugh, D Brooks. Seriously?* Not the person I wanted her to say.

D was a guy I dated earlier in college for a few months, but I had known him for years. We actually rode the school bus together in high school. I was a mature fourteen-year-old freshman. He was a dweeby fifteen-year-old sophomore who lived up the street. We used to sit in the very back two seats of the bus because we were the cool kids who got picked up first.

You really get to know someone when you're on a school bus for close to an hour every single day. One day, the dweeby kid from up the street asked me to "go steady," or whatever you do when you're fifteen. His question came along with a mix CD, complete with a typed label of all the artists and songs. It contained some of my favorites—Train's "Drops of Jupiter" and Dave Matthews Band's "The Space Between," to name a couple. Wow, how could I say no? Unfortunately for him, that's exactly what I did, but he let me keep the CD. Win-win! I ended up dating one of his best friends for more than a year, and Dweeby D turned into Mr. Popular, prom-court-participant, sports-star D. Needless to say, we weren't really friends after that. Round one done. Score: Rachael (1), D (0).

One random day in college years later, we ran into each other on campus, and sparks definitely flew. He asked for my number and said we should hang out. I was interested, and he actually called. Like a giddy schoolgirl, I was super excited for our date. He picked me up in his posh, green sedan, and off we went to dinner and a movie, *The Exorcism of Emily Rose*. How romantic. After our second date, we slept together, and I fell hard. Not sure what happened to the high school Rachael who just wanted the mix CD, but Dweeby D had swept me off my feet. We dated and slept together for about a month before I pushed the pivotal "what are we?" talk. It didn't exactly go as planned. He didn't want to be in a relationship, and thought we were just having fun. Ouch. D then proceeded to date a blonde bombshell for two years. Didn't want a relationship, my ass. Round two done. Score: Rachael (1), D (1). We were even.

So, when I heard Dweeby D was at the bar down the street, I was less than thrilled. I did learn, however, that he was newly single. Blonde bombshell didn't work out in the end. Bummer. After talking to Bestie, we decided to all meet up, and you'd think I would be somewhat proper. Nope, not even a little. Granted, alcohol was involved, but I proceeded to yell at him for over an hour. Apparently, our two-year hiatus left me with a lot to say—I mean, yell. Somehow, we ended up back at my apartment because *that* was a good idea, but we didn't sleep together. We slept in the same bed, and the next morning, I had a foggy memory of all the yelling that ensued the night before. Oops. I muttered an apology, and to my surprise D asked me for my number. *I'm sorry, what? I was mean and yelled! Yet he wants my phone number? Um, okay.*

I asked him what he was planning on doing with it, and he said he wanted to take me to dinner. I'm pretty sure my jaw fell off my face and hit the floor. Nonetheless, I gave him my number, and he actually called me that day. Not a week later, but the very day after I yelled at him.

What did I have to lose? At the minimum, I would have some decent conversation and a free dinner.

We ended up going to dinner the following week, and to many more dinners after that. Most amazing was that he never expected sex, even though we slept together years ago. After a month of dinners and dates, I decided to air my baggage—my airport full of baggage. We were lying in my bed, not having sex again, and I told him I needed to tell him something. Nothing to do with him, but something that happened to me.

Cue the verbal vomit: "So, about seven months ago, I was raped when I lived in Washington, DC, by this asshole masquerading as a cabbie. He was African American, and I was in his front seat, and he held a knife to my neck, and I thought I was gonna die. I tried to offer a blowjob, but he insisted on sex, and so that is what happened. Oh, and a few days ago, I had to be tested for HIV, again. Did you know that HIV can show up as much as a year later? I didn't. So I have to go get tested every few months. My mom calls and listens to the answering service for my results. This time, it was negative. Thank God, right? Okay, you can go now—run for the high hills—because I am really jaded and messed up beyond belief. Thank you for all the dates; it's been lovely."

Complete silence. The score was about to go up again, D (2), Rachael (1). We had a good run. But then the silence broke, and Dweeby D said he wasn't going anywhere. He was so devastated by what happened to me and couldn't apologize enough. He had a few questions, followed by a lot of questions, but he wasn't running.

Maybe yelling at him that first night was a blessing in disguise—he could handle anything from me now. Who was this guy? The kid on the back of the bus making mix CDs turned college heartbreaker turned mature twenty-something, who was now dating a rape victim. Apparently, third time's a charm, as the saying goes. One month turned into many months, which eventually turned into years, and Dweeby D is now my fabulous husband. We did have sex, but it was all on my time, and I will be forever grateful to him for that. He was the only person I had sex with after my attack, and who would have thought he would be my last?

Chapter 15
Therapy

⌒•••••••⌒

I'm a big fan of therapy—not only for a specific issue, but also for everyday sanity. Can't say I have ever made it to maintenance-level therapy, where I didn't have a specific issue or reason to go, but I'm a fan of it even so. Finding the right therapist is key and quite the selection process. It can feel like speed dating until you find the right one. My first therapist after the rape sucked. I didn't realize this until after I was done with her. Apparently, she specialized in victims of violence, but I became a victim of her therapy sessions. Joking . . . kind of. She wasn't gentle enough with me and would bluntly tell me I needed to do this and that, which I never ended up doing. However, talking to *someone* throughout grad school was better than talking to no one.

My sessions usually consisted of me crying about not having a boyfriend (before Dweeby D came back into the picture), crying about exams, crying about nothing, and more crying. Rarely did I actually talk about the rape. Initially I did, since that was the entire reason I was in therapy. But then I stopped and found myself talking about all these other problems. I always got the feeling the therapist didn't like it when I cried. Reason 432 why she sucked. I didn't care—crying was a big win for me since I didn't really cry when everything happened.

Basically, the therapist did enough for me to get through the year, so she did serve some purpose. Let's just say there were no tears of sadness or hugs at our last session. The rape still loomed in the background, but at the almost-one-year mark, I thought I was doing all right. *Thought* being the operative word.

Chapter 16
Mastered My Master's

Grad school: done. Not sure how the hell I did it, but I did, and I even came out of the year of hell with a new boyfriend. It was almost laughable. At the one-year mark (I prefer the word *mark* to *anniversary* as I equate anniversaries with happy things—weddings, relationships, weight loss—not rape), I hadn't heard anything about my case and honestly thought I never would. I started to come to terms with the fact that I had done everything I could, and I had to let it go. Some good news: I went for my last round of blood testing shortly before my master's graduation, and I officially did not have HIV. What a fucking sigh of relief if I ever did have one! I could at least have some closure on that piece of this whole thing.

I moved back home with my parents for a few months before starting my full-time job with the same accounting firm I had interned for in—wait for it—Washington, DC. Yes, I was moving back to the scene of the crime at the end of the summer. Was I crazy? Yes. But my hometown Raleigh office was so small at the time that they weren't taking graduates right out of college. So back to the DC area it was. I wanted to live in a completely different city this time, so I decided to move to Arlington, Virginia. Granted it was still close to the District, but it had a new atmosphere. If I never again in my life had to see where Shithead dropped me off in Alexandria, that would be ideal. It would be all right . . . right?

In the few months of living at home, I got super skinny. I'm talking hot girl, cover of a magazine skinny. I joined Weight Watchers, and I was a fanatic about it. I was never considered obese, but I wanted to be smaller. It became my new obsession, in a good way most of the time. I directed my energy into running, eating well, and weighing myself once a week. Down and down the numbers on the scale went. It was exhilarating and I had complete control over it. My days consisted of working out and studying for the dreaded certified public accountant (CPA) exam by day and hanging with D and friends by night. I even got a part-time babysitting gig to help pay for my first month's rent in Arlington.

Life was actually going okay. I had my plan and felt like I was kind of back on track, and I was now thirty pounds lighter. I could literally wear whatever I wanted and, for the first time in a while, felt good about it. By the time September rolled around, I had convinced myself I could indeed move back to Virginia and start my job, which is exactly what I did. I found a roommate (who became a knower, per my rule, and ultimately a great friend) on Craigslist, of all places, and we had a kickass two-bedroom apartment. She was also from North Carolina, and we had grown up relatively close to one another, so we hit it off instantly. She was in a long-distance relationship as well, and we both didn't know many people in Virginia.

My mom and I painted my bedroom a putrid green, because apparently that was in style in 2009. We stocked up on everything Ikea and got it perfect before my debut as a businesswoman. I started my new job along with twenty-five of my peers and got my first paycheck, which was more money than I had ever seen come into my bank account. Face had pretty much morphed into my real self—while I was sober, at least—and the rape became a tad bit more of a distant memory. I was all right.

Of course, this didn't last long. Why would it? Everything was about to blow wide open again, and I never saw it coming.

Chapter 17
The Call That Changed It All

It was a new year and time for a fresh start. After a two-week Christmas break, I geared up for my first official busy season as a tax accountant. I didn't really know at the time what that entailed, but I was ready. Come to find out, busy season consisted of working sixtyish hours a week on average from January to April, canceling any and all weekend plans to the point where you just didn't make them, and leaving the office to have a dinner break, only to sign back on to your laptop for more work at home shortly thereafter.

Ignorance was bliss. It was January 7, 2010, a typical Thursday. I drove my ridiculously long commute to work due to the insanity that was DC traffic, got some coffee, said my hellos to my fellow busy-season first-timers, and sat down at my desk.

At about 9 a.m., my BlackBerry vibrated with a 202 area code number I didn't recognize. *Eh, I guess I should answer it. Maybe it's someone on my team or a client? Would my client be calling me, an associate only three months in? Probably not.* But I answered.

A woman said on the other end, "Hello, this is Detective Z. Is Rachael Ostrowski available?" I froze. I thought I was speaking; however, no words came out of my mouth.

"This is she," I finally said, in a broken, old-man crackly-sounding voice.

Detective Z (Z, as I will call her) said, "Yes, hi, I have been newly assigned to your sexual assault case reported back in 2008. We found a match in the system from your DNA rape kit and would like to meet with you to discuss a few things."

You know that ringing sound in your ears you get after a super loud noise? A blaring fire engine drives by, or fireworks erupt on the Fourth of July, or a smoke alarm accidentally goes off in your house because you burned the chocolate chip cookies? That's the sound I heard. Everything around me was moving in slow motion. The voices around my cubicle were like muffled robots, the words on my computer screen were blurred, and I wasn't sure I had heard this woman correctly. My rape kit had been tested? There was a match? The man who destroyed me had been identified? *No, this can't be true.* It was 9 a.m. on January 7; I was supposed to be checking email and looking at trial balances to plug into pro-forma Excel workbooks so my tax team could estimate extension payments for our client. I was *not* supposed to be on the phone with a detective.

"Hello, Rachael, are you there?" Z questioned.

"Um, yes, yes, sorry, I am here. I really can't believe this. Who did it? What is the guy's name?" I stammered.

"Unfortunately, we can't divulge that information to you at this time, but we would like to meet with you to discuss further."

Can't divulge? Why the fuck not? I am the victim here! Shouldn't I be informed immediately? Is this guy in custody? Does he know who I am? My mind was exploding. *I should probably go into an office behind a closed door.* No one was a knower at work at that point. Sadly, my friend who had interned with me a year and half ago had transferred to the Atlanta office. But I never thought I would receive this phone call, so it was a non-issue. I was supposed to be done with this. Moving on, right?

Wrong. I stumbled into an office with a door that would close, and the detective and I agreed on a time and place to meet that day.

"Thank you for your time," Z wrapped up. And *click*, the phone call was over.

What a morning. God, it's only the morning. What the hell is happening? What do I do now? My client trial balances dropped to the bottom of my priority list. I needed to call my mom, I needed to call D, and I needed to talk to HR. I couldn't live in this godforsaken city. Who was I kidding by moving back up here? After talking and crying my way through phone calls with D and my mom, I stumbled to my HR manager's office, dizzy from the shock of it all. My HR manager was someone different now that I was a full-time employee, so she had no clue what was in store for her. I walked in, shut the door, and she immediately knew something wasn't right. I proceeded to tell her everything, in my verbal-vomit fashion that I tended to default to when sharing this series of events. I ended with, "I need to transfer to the Raleigh, North Carolina, office as soon as humanly possible." *Whoa, once again, what the hell is happening?* The HR manager was blown away. She could barely form words. This was certainly not what she expected on a Thursday in early January. As with most people, she was devastated for me and extremely apologetic. No offense to her—I was appreciative of her kind words—but I needed to get the hell out of this city, and I needed her to make that happen for me. I had gone into crisis mode and needed to take action. She explained she would talk with her HR counterpart in the Carolinas market and get back to me with next steps. The transferring process was no easy feat. It ended up taking close to eight long, drawn-out months for me to make it back down to North Carolina. EIGHT MONTHS. Any longer, and I was throwing out an ultimatum: either I worked on my current client remotely in the Raleigh office, or I was out.

Those eight months, as you can imagine, were nothing less than a complete catastrophe. But let me back up so I can paint the full picture.

Chapter 18
Detective Z

Somehow, I made it through that workday. Later, sitting and staring at the coffee shop and delaying my inevitable entrance, my mind went crazy again. *What exactly will I be walking into? Is it going to be an interrogation like the first time?* Hopefully not, given they had supposedly identified Shithead, so there was truth to my claims.

Deciding I'd had enough with my thoughts, I mustered the courage to go inside, where Detective Z was sitting at a table off to the left. I would not have known who she was had it not been for who she was with: Detective Dickhead #2, the asshole who sat in the back seat of the squad car that morning and would not stop telling me that I was drunk and confused about the rape. It was precisely the reunion I was looking for. *How confused and drunk do I look now?* Coincidentally, our meeting spot coffee shop happened to be none other than a Starbucks. Go figure. I thought about offering to get his partner a coffee and a muffin, just for old time's sake.

I slowly walked toward them, my nerves now at an all-time high. Detective Z greeted me and started by thanking me for coming. She then explained that Detective Dickhead #1, the curb-parking Starbucks fanatic, was no longer involved. *WHAT A FUCKING BUMMER.* This was quite the silver lining to January 7. One dickhead down, one to go. Rather than firing off my never-ending list of questions, I let Z take the lead. She said that they knew who Shithead was, and my providing his

DNA was what did the trick. *Well, at least that wasn't all for nothing.*

"So, what's this guy's name?" I asked, not able to contain myself. Z couldn't give it to me, which I still to this day don't quite understand. Then again, I also don't quite understand how the justice system could be so fucked up. So there's that.

"Is he in custody? Or is he at least off the street?" I asked.

Z replied, "We can't say."

My favorite response. *Okay, so I don't get to know his name or where he is, fine. Please, Detective Z, tell me what I can know, since I'm only the victim after all.* I thought this should be a pretty open and shut case. DNA? Check. Perpetrator? Presumably in custody. Victim? Willing to testify. I could not have been more wrong and was about to encounter the first hurdle of this case: determining jurisdiction.

My little drive with Detective Dickheads #1 and #2 came back to haunt me. Apparently, the fact that I couldn't recall the exact location where my rape occurred was a major issue—much larger than I could have ever imagined, and much larger than it ever should have been. Jurisdiction determined which state (or District) would take the case. Would it be Virginia? Or Washington, DC? I reported it to the lovely sexual assault unit in our nation's capital, but because the rape could have taken place in Virginia, the two courts had to battle it out. As Detective Z explained all of this to me, I gazed over at the still-present Dickhead #2. He looked bored. *Come on, man, make eye contact with me.* He did, for a fleeting moment, and then immediately looked away. I would be embarrassed too, like a dog with its tail between its legs kind of embarrassed. He majorly screwed up, and he knew he did. He would never admit it, though. He was the type of guy who would never compromise his pride to admit guilt.

Back to the jurisdiction issue: How hard could it be to determine? Couldn't someone just flip a coin? Pick a location out of a hat? I didn't know where it happened and never would. Detective Z stated the issue wouldn't be resolved that day, which obviously I knew. That was pretty much all the information I got on January 7: *You caught Shithead, but you can't tell me his name, and he could be charged, but you can't move forward with it because of jurisdiction.* Fantastic, and oh so helpful.

I will say, though, I liked Detective Z. She was a woman, first off. Up to that point I had only experienced unsavory dealings with male officers, so having a female detective was quite refreshing and reassuring that I did indeed make the right decision to report. Not to play the man-hating card, but with regard to law enforcement, I did. I needed someone to believe me and not interrogate the shit out of me. She did both. Shortly after our awkward eye contact, Detective Dickhead #2 had to leave. God bless whomever he went to help or save that day. Or maybe he didn't really have to leave. Maybe he wanted to. Maybe my daggering glare did him in. Probably the latter. Coward.

After he left, I asked Z if I could make a request. I wanted Detective Dickhead #2 to be taken off the case. I gave her the skinny version of my initial experience with him the day of the rape. Mortified, she apologized and said she would take care of it, making it the second silver lining of January 7. Second dickhead down. Looking back, I should have reported those two detectives. If I had any regrets throughout this entire mess, this was it. I wish I had reamed their asses with a lawsuit for putting me through the ringer the way they did. Yeah, yeah, I get they had a job to do. However, I would bet their job description never mentioned anything about revictimizing the victim over and over again or making a pit stop for a coffee and a muffin.

Snapping back to reality, the meeting was over.

That morning, I woke up for an ordinary day at the beginning of busy season. That evening, I left a Starbucks with a new detective on my case, the case I never thought I would hear about again. As much as I loathed the initial detectives, I reported it. I reported what happened to me, provided DNA, and something actually came of it. I didn't know much at that point, but it was something. Leaving, I felt weird. I was angry this had resurfaced, but relieved Shithead had been identified. I was hopeful my case would be resolved, but uneasy about the whole jurisdictional issue. Again, I wanted to shout from the rooftops, but also hide behind Face. So many emotions erupted all over again.

Chapter 19
Pause

C an we all take a minute to realize that it took a year and a half for my rape kit to be tested? That's eighteen months, or 547 days, give or take. All of that DNA just sat there, boxed up, probably on one of those big metal shelves like you see in *Law & Order*, collecting dust. What's most disturbing is that a year and a half is nothing. That is considered good turnaround time, especially in a big city. How lucky was I? I can't imagine getting that phone call five, ten years later. Eighteen months was bad enough.

The nation's rape kit backlog is despicable. Speaking of *Law & Order*, *SVU*'s leading actress, Mariska Hargitay, is a major advocate for ending sexual violence. She wrote an opinion article for *CNN* in 2018 that mirrors to a T my thoughts on the nation's backlog. One of her most powerful quotes that really resonates with me is the following:

> *Beyond the obvious threat to public safety, beyond the wasted opportunities to both prosecute the guilty and exonerate the wrongly convicted, the backlog sends a devastating and inexcusable message to survivors: You don't matter. What happened to you doesn't matter.*

Now, if that does not make your blood boil, I do not know what will. It is not that the police cannot keep up with rape kit testing. In some instances, the police flat out do not believe victims, so they get rid of the rape kits. Hargitay states, "A detective in North Carolina authorized the trashing of a rape kit a month after it was collected from a woman who was gang raped because the investigator didn't believe her." What the hell? And in my home state, nonetheless. I cannot say enough how baffling our justice system is. It is absolutely disgusting.

The fact of the matter is that rapes get put at the bottom of the barrel in most cases. Rapes are not murders. Murders are typically investigated immediately because there is a murderer on the loose. If there are no resolutions, the cases go cold. You never hear about murder cases being backlogged. Detectives would lose their jobs. Instead, detectives will spend their careers trying to solve murder cases. Rapes may as well be cold right from the start.

Think about this: How many murderers do we hear about who are also rapists? Several. And how many times do we hear, "Well, if we had caught that guy after he raped that woman, this murder would have never happened?" Several. Food for thought. All of this is my own humble opinion and experience. If police departments can't handle the influx of rape kits, get more police. If money is the issue, get more money. Someone must fight for these changes. Something must change; it is completely ridiculous and infuriating.

Hargitay's article mentions, "[The] National Institute for Justice issued recommendations for best practices about the counting, tracking, and testing of rape kits, reforms that the federal government agrees are needed." Isn't that promising? I'm so glad the federal government agrees that the simple testing of rape kits is needed. Again, what the hell? She goes on to say, "In order to be able to hold jurisdictions accountable, those recommendations must become law in all 50 states." These protocols aren't already laws across the nation? Are you fucking kidding me? My rape occurred in 2008. And in 2018, basic laws such as requiring the testing of rape kits don't even exist in all fifty states.

In 2018, North Carolina state investigators learned that there were more than 15,000 rape kits that were never tested. The state's attorney general confirmed my thoughts about where my rape kit sat—on "local law enforcement shelves all across the state." You have to figure this is the same across most jurisdictions. It leaves me speechless, which is incredibly hard to do. North Carolina is currently proposing the "Survivor Act" in 2019, which consists of legislation to prioritize the testing of sexual assault kits across the state. This act makes the following actions mandatory:

Immediate notification to law enforcement;

Required testing;

Outsourcing kits to private labs as funds are available; and

Combined DNA Index System (CODIS) database hit follow-ups.

So at least they are finally putting this at the top of their to-do list. While, yes, it is something to celebrate that this is finally happening, it also truly shows that *nothing* was being done beforehand. Again, the fact that these protocols were not already laws makes my blood boil. It only took 15,000 backlogged rape kits to get here—absolutely ridiculous. Furthermore, as of early 2019, North Carolina has already tested 800 of those 15,000 kits. Of those 800, more than 10 percent came back with hits in the CODIS database. That's eighty-seven cases in which a perpetrator has been identified. Eighty-seven victims who have been waiting and waiting for their cases to be solved. Eighty-seven victims who went through what I went through but received no closure.

How does one even go about making that call? I imagine it would go something like this: "Yes, hello there, my apologies, but your rape kit didn't really matter back in the day and it has been sitting on a dusty police department shelf . . . until now." It's so incredibly fucked up. My heart goes out to each and every one of those victims—may they all find the closure they need and deserve.

While it is ludicrous that the possibility even existed, I am so thankful the District of Columbia happened to be one of those jurisdictions that didn't trash my rape kit; Detective Dickheads sure as hell didn't believe me. Someone with a heart and a brain was looking out for me that day.

Chapter 20
Four Months

Would you believe it took four MONTHS—not hours, not days, not weeks, but four months—for these jurisdictions to decide *which* jurisdiction would try my case? I have absolutely no idea what went into this decision or how it was made. All I know is that every few days, I checked in with Detective Z for an update. And every few days, the update was the same: they were working on it, and she couldn't tell me anything more at this time. I began to think we were back in 2008 when I knew nothing about the case because my case might as well have been nonexistent at that point.

I tried to focus on my job, because, oh right, I had one of those. Busy season sucked. It was one of those situations where you don't really know what you are getting into until you are deep in the mud. I spent every free moment I had either thinking about the case or actively trying not to think about it; therefore, I was always thinking about it. I welcomed Face back into the picture. Not that it ever left; it had just become the norm and not as difficult to put on. However, now that my case had resurfaced, my secret was back in the forefront. I had to work a bit harder to ensure Face was doing its job.

In the midst of busy season and my pending case, I decided it was a good idea to take the last section of the CPA exam, because why not pile everything on at once? Working all day, trying to squeeze in study breaks here and there, and then studying a few hours at night was exhausting. By the grace of God, I had already passed the other three sections. As ready as I was going to be, I took a day off work, said a small prayer, and took that test. A few weeks later, there was another silver lining (always trying my best to find those little suckers) to all the shit going on around me. I got home to my apartment exceptionally late one night, and I decided to get the mail. A few coupon booklets and a few envelopes—I thought it was all junk until I saw one that looked like a car insurance offer. Thankfully, I opened it. It was a letter from the North Carolina Certified Public Accountancy Board; the state hadn't gotten with the times yet and still sent information via snail mail. I respect that—the build-up and anticipation about killed me, but it made for more excitement when I started reading.

The top line of the letter read, "Congratulations, you have passed the CPA exam." Holy shit! Once again, I had surprised myself. Finishing grad school was far-fetched, but I did it, and now I was going to be Rachael Ostrowski, CPA. It sounded a hell of a lot better than Rachael Ostrowski, rape victim. I was very proud of myself. I called my mom at midnight because I just couldn't wait to tell her. This of course freaked her out, and she answered the phone in a panic, but it was worth it. We were both screaming and laughing in disbelief. Standardized tests and I did not always get along. We also called my grandmother—who was a night owl, so she was awake—to share the news. More happy screaming and congratulatory words. It was a great end to a long busy season day.

Pressing on, I was finally on the receiving end of an update call. A decision had been made, almost four months to the day after January 7. Drum roll, please . . . The District of Columbia was going to take my case. I wondered what the deciding factor was. Did Virginia want to maintain their current rape statistics? Did the District have more manpower? I didn't really give a damn; I was elated to be over that hurdle. So, now that we had a place, what was next?

Finding out information was like slowly peeling back the layers of an onion. Jurisdiction is the skin. Once the skin is gone, you are left with this shiny, almost iridescent bulb just waiting to reveal its core. The only way to do that is by carefully peeling back all the layers. With each layer, the eye burn gets a bit more intense. The police were holding my shiny bulb with all of those informational layers; the first layer took the shine of my onion right off.

Chapter 21
The First Layer

꿈·····················

You don't know what you don't know. All I knew at that point was there was this nameless guy who raped me, and the courts decided it took place in Washington, DC. Next up came one hell of a layer. Shithead was already in prison in Virginia. For what? He was a serial rapist and used weapons to commit the rapes. Including me, four women total, all around the same age, had come forward. Two of those cases went to trial, and Shithead was found guilty in both. One of his rapes occurred in 2006. Perhaps if the rape kit backlog was not such a prevalent issue, Shithead would have been caught in 2006, and his three additional victims could have been spared. But there absolutely had to have been more than four of us. The Rape, Abuse, and Incest National Network (RAINN) reports that, on average, one in five college-age women will report a rape. To break that down, if there were four of us who reported, Shithead statistically had raped twenty women. Twenty. Well, shit.

Who was telling all of this to me? A prosecuting attorney (Attorney, as I shall call him) who worked for the US attorney general's office in DC. Why was a United States attorney the one telling me this news, you ask? Because my case was now being considered a federal case due to the fact that Shithead would need to be transferred across state lines anytime there was a hearing. There you have it, *The United States vs. Shithead.* I was dealing with a *major* criminal here. This wasn't just some guy who randomly decided to pick me up one night and have some fun. He had done this before and had perfected his little game. It does not get much more grotesque than that.

That ringing sound in my ears, the one from January 7, came back as I sat in this conference room in the freaking US attorney general's office. All the walls were white, and we were at this dark wooden table with about twenty-two chairs crammed around it. *Jesus, how big are the meetings in this room? Can everyone sit comfortably at this table?* I was slightly concerned, especially if someone struggled with claustrophobia. My curiosity provided a nice two-second mental break from the information I was just told. Thankfully my mom had come up to DC and was present at the unveiling of this first layer of craziness with me. It was an "I'll put on the fudge" situation, which we fully intended to enjoy after this little meeting.

"Okay, so you're telling me that Shithead forcibly raped multiple women while using a weapon of his choice?" I questioned as I struggled to wrap my head around this.

"Correct," Attorney replied.

We had so many questions: When did these other rapes occur? Who were the other women? Were they okay? Did Shithead kill anyone? What did this mean for my case? My mom and I fired these questions off like pinballs at the arcade. *Pow, pow, ping.* More information meant more power, and my God did we need some power in all of this.

Not surprisingly, we received minimal information. Attorney could only shed light on the fact that this guy wasn't out walking the streets, which was peace of mind, don't get me wrong. It was like Attorney was dangling a little carrot in front of my face, and now I wanted to eat the whole damn garden.

I will say that Attorney was the second person involved in this case who I liked. He was not representing me, but he definitely had my best interests in mind. Finally, someone else was on my side. Attorney was youngish and completely bald. The baldness added to his badass-ness. He was quick on his feet and went to law school in my neck of the woods back in North Carolina, so our bond was pretty immediate. Hands down,

Attorney was the first person to make me feel 100 percent comfortable about everything that happened. Well, not comfortable in a cozying-up-on-the-couch kind of comfortable—the type of comfortable where I wasn't being judged. He believed me and was going to fight for me, and I needed that from someone outside of my knowers.

We peeled back one layer of the onion, so now what? Attorney explained the overview of the process. I joked, "So this isn't going to be wrapped up in an hour, like on *Law & Order*?" We all chuckled, then returned to being serious.

No, it wasn't going to take an hour; in fact, it was going to take hundreds of hours. The first step would be testifying to a grand jury to get my rapist indicted. *I'm sorry, come again? Even with all of Shithead's DNA I provided—his semen was found on me, for the love of God—he still needs to be indicted?* Oh, the many ways I love (but really hate) our justice system. Innocent until proven guilty, regardless of all the evidence. Before you can even think about a trial, one must go through the indictment bullshit.

Attorney explained that a grand jury is kind of like a trial jury, but there are more people—approximately twenty-three, give or take a few. Another difference is that there is no cross-examination. The prosecution presents and questions the witnesses, and the grand jury decides if there is *probable* cause that a person committed a crime. How informative. Didn't ever think I would need to know the inner workings of our court system, but there we were.

One word stuck out to me in Attorney's lesson in law: *Witnesses*.

Chapter 22
Witnesses

Witnesses could only mean one thing: I was not going to be the only one to testify to the grand jury. I needed others to corroborate my story and make my case the strongest it could be. Who would those others be? Cuz and Boyfriend. *Fuck.* I hadn't talked to Boyfriend since the end of the summer of doom. Cuz still didn't know. She had become a great friend, one of my best. *How will she react?*

It was almost two years ago at that point. I didn't want to hurt her because my not telling her honestly didn't have anything to do with her as a person. It was mainly because I didn't know her at the time, or if I could trust her. I obviously learned I could trust her, but as more and more time passed, the harder it became to tell her, so I continued withholding my horrifying secret. Little did I know, this decision would land me in quite the dilemma. Attorney presented me with two options: I could tell Cuz, and she could willingly come to the grand jury to testify, or I could not tell Cuz, and she would be subpoenaed to testify to the grand jury. *Fuck, I don't like either of those.* There was no way in hell I was going to have her find out this information from a damn subpoena, so I opted to tell her myself. I also wanted to track down Boyfriend to tell him the latest and greatest, and that he would be receiving a call from Attorney.

Leaving the US attorney general's office, I felt pummeled. I felt like the quarterback who got sacked in a football game, fumbled the ball, and by the time he stood up, the other team had run it down the field for a touchdown. How could this be my life? I never thought I would set foot in the US attorney general's office in Washington, DC.

Nevertheless, I had business to take care of. I immediately called Cuz and casually asked if she could come over to my apartment. She was able to come the next day. *Phew*. I didn't know the timeline for when Cuz could be subpoenaed—shocking, I know—so I had to tell her as soon as possible.

When Cuz got to my apartment, she could tell something was up. I couldn't ignore it any longer. We sat on my Rooms To Go couch that I was super proud of because it was my first adult, non-college purchase. It was cream colored and velvety and quite comfortable. We sat there, and I felt the verbal vomit coming, but I worked hard to contain it.

I started out slowly. "So, you remember that night we first hung out back in 2008 . . ."

Cuz said, "Yes, yes, I do" with tremendous hesitation and a look of *what the hell are you about to tell me?*

A bomb, Cuz, so brace yourself. I continued, and it all came pouring out. The verbal vomit was merely delayed. There was silence, and Cuz dropped her head in her hands and wept. We sat together on my velvety couch, sobbing. She was in disbelief. She then asked the question I dreaded most: "Why didn't you tell me right when it happened?!"

I explained that I simply couldn't. It was all so fucked up, and I didn't want *that* to be her memory of me that night. Even though now it was.

I explained that this was absolutely not the way I intended on telling her, but I needed her help. I really can't imagine what that must have felt like: "Hey, remember that night in 2008 when we had a drunken blast? Well, I was raped afterward, and now I need you to go testify about every detail you can recall from that night, almost two years ago. Thanks!"

There is essentially no *right* way to receive that type of information, but she handled it all amazingly. She wasn't mad that I didn't initially tell her; she was just completely blown away. She really wished she could have helped me through it all, and I was so appreciative. But bottom line was I had only just met her, and she understood that. She 100 percent agreed to testify and just needed to know when and where. One of the best things about Cuz, still to this day, is that you can call her and tell her you need her, and she's there, no questions asked. That's what she did that day. I called, she came, she listened, and she was ready to take action. One witness down. One to go.

I can't remember if I called or emailed Boyfriend. I think it was an email. The gist was basically, "Hey, long time no talk! Hope you are doing well, yada yada yada. Not to put a huge damper on your life, but they found the dude who attacked me, and I just wanted to give you a heads-up. You are going to be receiving a call from an attorney because you are considered a witness in my case. Because you are a witness, you are going to have to testify to a grand jury about that night and the following day to corroborate my story. I really do hope you are doing well."

Again, not quite sure what that must have felt like. "Hey, remember that one random Saturday almost two years ago when your girlfriend was raped? Yeah? Okay, now you must recall every detail from that night and testify to a room full of random people." Fuck.

Boyfriend replied almost immediately thanking me for the heads-up. He was willing to help in any way he could, and I honestly didn't expect anything different. Through it all, he was a good guy and we were young. We were too young to be dealing with such adult matters. Nothing really went our way that summer, and such is life. He came through for me, and I am forever grateful to him for that.

Chapter 23
A Call of My Own

Amid all the chaos, I randomly decided one day that *I* was going to make a phone call of my own. To whom, you may wonder? It was to none other than Detective Dickhead #1. Unfortunately for him, I still had his phone number from the day he told me "all of this," a.k.a., the rape, was going to blow over and be fine. He was about to wish he had never given it to me.

I sat in my car and hit send. It rang and rang. *He probably isn't going to answer.* I imagined he was off making someone else's life a living hell. *Well, at least I had the courage to even dial,* I thought. But then, a "hella" on the other end. A "hell-a," not a "hell-o," like he was irritated that he was even getting a phone call. Typical.

I proceeded, "Um, yes, hi, is this Detective Dickhead #1?" I used his actual name, of course, but it would have been lovely to use my nickname for him.

He responded, "Yeah . . . it is."

I responded, "Oh, perfect. My name is Rachael Ostrowski—you may not remember me, but you worked my rape case a few years back and—"

He interrupted, "Yes, I remember you." Silence. *Is he going to elaborate on his memory at all? I guess not.*

I replied, "Great, okay. Well, I just wanted to let you know that you were wrong that day. My rape did happen, and my rapist has been caught.

I just thought you should know."

Click. Son of a bitch hung up on me. Not that I was surprised. I wasn't even mad. I said exactly what I wanted to say, and he heard it. I smiled and went about my day feeling empowered and badass.

Chapter 24
The In-Between

One may wonder how I was *actually* doing through all of this. The truth? Sober, I was handling it all right. I was on meds for anxiety and depression, as I had been for a while. They didn't cure all my mental issues, but they certainly helped. I was going about life, wearing Face, doing my job, carrying on a somewhat normal relationship with D. At times, it got scarier, with some serious thoughts of suicide. I sometimes wondered what would happen if I just ingested the whole bottle of pills. Would I wake up? Or would I just get the best sleep of my life? Who would find me? I was always able to reason myself out of it. I honestly don't think I would have acted on it, as I think suicide is incredibly selfish. But the thoughts were there, and they were dark.

When I was drunk, I was a hot mess. Actually, hot mess was an understatement. I was a disaster. Drinking became my therapy. I was seeing a real therapist in Virginia, who was worlds better than the one I saw in Chapel Hill, thank the Lord, but on the weekends, alcohol was my therapist. Oh, how I loved my weekend therapist.

I was definitely a social drinker. You would rarely find me drinking alone in my apartment, which was certainly a good thing. I wanted a crowd to join me so I wouldn't be the only one. If everyone wanted to drink, that meant I could too. Except that everyone else's idea of a good time tended to be a bit different than mine. While most of our crowd drank to get drunk, I drank to black out. I drank to forget what was happening in my sober life. I drank to let loose and be free and take Face off. I never had a problem finding someone who would drink with me. D drove up to DC or I drove down to Raleigh almost every weekend, so I could always look forward to my weekend therapy.

My alcohol of choice was just about anything. Maybe I would start with liquor, a shot even, then have some beer, while getting ready for the night—that pre-gaming ritual I loved. Once we were out on the town, though, it was game over. I could never be without a drink. I'd sometimes go up to the bar by myself, order two beers, chug one, and then walk back to the group as if I had only ordered one. Sneaky, I know. I needed to get wasted, and I needed it to happen quickly—especially on Fridays because I was reeling from the workweek, and probably some case bullshit. Round after round after round until, to my dismay, the bar was closing, and it was time to go home. Ending the night was always the worst, and it was at that point that I tended to black out and forget how the night ended.

On numerous occasions, Bestie would accompany D up to DC for some shenanigans. She was a knower and one of the few people I trusted to see me in my blacked-out state. She and D were usually the ones to recount the events of nights past in the morning. Two stories, out of the countless, still stick with me today.

The first involved a typical night out, and it was before I had learned that Shithead was in jail, but after I knew they had identified him. Bestie and D were visiting. Bestie's boyfriend at the time also lived in the District, which meant more people to add to my drinking crowd. Solid. I was in it to win it that night. Weekend therapy was in full swing and blacking out was a definite. At the end of the night, we needed to ride the metro to get back to my apartment. Bestie's boyfriend had no idea about the rape. Apparently—because I don't recall doing this—when I stepped onto the metro, there was a black man sitting opposite the door I had just walked through. I sat down across from him, staring. Glaring, even. In my delirious state, I made up my mind that he was Shithead.

I got up, stumbled over next to my crew and, whispering at first, started saying, "That's him, that's the man who did it. That's him!" The whispering slowly grew to a talking voice, and, thankfully, before I could get into a full-blown shout, Bestie and D calmed me down. The sense of calm didn't last long. By that point the black man had exited the metro, luckily for him. I then insisted we had to go find him. He was the one who raped me, and he just got off the metro. We had to find him!

I'm pretty sure I was shouting at that point, with no awareness of who else was on the metro. I was fixated on this black guy, who probably had a good job, mowed his lawn, had a wife and kids, and was just trying to get home after a night out. Again, I didn't care. I created hell for those with me, but I knew I was going to be okay because Bestie and D were with me. I also ended up telling my whole debacle to Bestie's boyfriend, because of course he needed to know what was going on, and that my rapist was just on the metro. We were all in danger! But we weren't.

Finally, the metro dinged at our stop. Bestie and her boyfriend were most likely sober at that point. My tirade was quite sobering, as you could imagine. They carried me back to my apartment like a player who got injured on the football field, got me inside, and I started up again. D always received the brunt of my yelling. Why didn't he go find Shithead? I saw him! He was right there on the metro, and D let him go!

As I sobbed uncontrollably while yelling, there was really nothing anyone could do. At least I was no longer in public, right? Silver lining? At one point, I wanted to leave my apartment and go find Shithead myself. If they weren't going to help me, I would do it myself. D had to block the door. I was one step away from physically trying to remove him from my path. Unsuccessful in my escape attempts, the night eventually ended with Bestie and D practically pinning me down on my bed and shushing me to sleep. What had started out as a fun night out ended as a hellacious nightmare. *I* was the hellacious nightmare.

It's weird because that was how the night of the rape began; the only difference was that Boyfriend and I were in a massive fight that evening. The night started out great, fun, carefree. It ended up as a hellacious nightmare, but Shithead was the hellacious nightmare *that* night.

The next morning, I didn't remember a thing. I looked at D, and realized another episode of Raging Rachael must have gone down. *Fuck.* That's typically how it went. I would wake up feeling hungover as shit and immediately cringe depending on the look on D's face. *Was Rachael a raging lunatic the night before or was she rational?* The answer was almost always the former. I would apologize profusely and promise to work on it. It's true what they say—we hurt the ones we love most. D was always my punching bag because I knew he wasn't going anywhere. He stayed, even with all my baggage, all my drunken episodes, all my breakdowns. I don't know how he stayed through all the Raging Rachael nights, but he did.

The second major standout story involved a similar night out, this time ending with a cab ride home. I was quite skeptical of cabs. Perhaps it was the fact that the one and only other time I had ridden in a "cab" in Washington, DC, I was raped at knifepoint. Yeah, that was probably it. So, when I realized the night was ending with a cab ride home, blacked-out Raging Rachael lost her shit.

That cabbie had no clue what type of ride he was about to embark on. Upon entering the cab, the yelling and sobbing began. Of course, I had my crew with me—all knowers, including D—so deep down I knew they would do their best to take care of me. I tried to get out of the cab. I couldn't stop screaming obscenities at the cab driver, going so far as to accuse him of being Shithead. Meanwhile, my crew was trying to talk me down and apologize to the cabbie. What a freaking mess. It was pretty much the same scenario back at my apartment: the threatening to leave, screaming at the top of my lungs at D to get out and to leave me alone, having to physically be put down to sleep, waking up, cringing, the whole nine yards. It sadly became all too predictable. I would have pep talks with myself on a Friday morning if I knew we were going out that night. I would tell myself, *Please don't let Raging Rachael come out tonight. Let's have a Rational Rachael night instead.* The pep talks rarely worked. If I had a Rational Rachael night, it was very soon followed by a Raging Rachael night.

I knew the drinking was bad, but it was my escape. As much as I knew I was hurting my crew, I still did it. It consumed me with guilt because it was almost out of my control. I would go into an evening with full belief that I was not going to black out, but then I would hit the point of no return and all hell would break loose. Yet D stayed.

The downward spiral was vicious and extremely scary. I watched myself fall deeper and deeper down a tunnel of doom, yet I tried to convince myself I was totally fine. During the week, I behaved. I would get up on time for work, get through busy-season days, wear Face, and give everyone a chance to forgive me for whatever I did the weekend before. Telltale sign of a problem: trying to rationalize and make sense of the non-problem. *I'm not drinking during the week, so I do have it under control.*

Someone very close to me was an alcoholic. I never thought it was a major issue, but after the drinking stopped, this person revealed it was a huge issue. They shared that sometimes they would disguise beer in a to-go coffee mug in the car and most days would empty the beer fridge after work. I, however, wasn't doing those things, so in my mind my drinking wasn't a major issue. But it was.

In life, I think we tend to look at others' bad behaviors to make ourselves feel better about our own, whether we do it consciously or subconsciously. In my case, I did it quite often because I desperately needed to feel better about my life and know that what I was doing was okay. This notion allowed me to justify my coping mechanism, which was drinking. In truth, I was so far from fine it became laughable, but I continued to hide it exceptionally well.

I strategically left out details of my weekend therapy during my sober therapy sessions. I was not at all ready to admit my methods of survival and how far into the tunnel of doom I was. I used drinking as a crutch and an excuse to escape. I compartmentalized and blocked out the rape when sober. So, I was essentially faking my way through sober therapy, which was probably not the best idea. Sober therapy definitely helped get me through my day-to-day life, don't get me wrong. But I wasn't necessarily getting better. Drinking made me feel like I could breathe and actually *feel*. Of course, this all worsened when my case blew back open and remained stagnant for months because of the fucking jurisdiction issue.

Looking back, I was extremely hard on myself. The drinking was not good. I know that. Perhaps this is just more justification, but I could have gone in a thousand different directions. I didn't turn to *hard* drugs, like smoking crack or shooting up heroin. I didn't turn into a sex addict. I didn't lose my job or become homeless. Somehow, I didn't push away all my friends and family. It could have been much worse, but I didn't exactly realize that at the time.

Chapter 25
The Grand Jury

It was July, and we had passed the two-year mark of the rape. I was about to testify to a grand jury in order to convince them that Shithead *probably* raped me. As the grand jury is the precursor to a trial, it only takes into consideration the validity of the accusation and whether criminal charges should be brought. I had gone through some preparation with Attorney so I wouldn't be caught completely off guard. Anyone testifying to a grand jury is going to be taken off guard, but I emphasize the *completely* part, as Attorney did take the edge off a little bit. He was good like that. I had my whole posse with me for the big day at the courthouse: my mom, D, Detective Z, and Attorney. Cuz and Boyfriend were going to be there at some point that day as well, but I didn't know when. Surprise, surprise, I didn't get to know any of that additional information. I was just the victim, after all, no big deal.

The courthouse was devastatingly bland with its beige floors, beige walls, and popcorn ceilings. It looked incredibly dated, as if it were pulled straight from a 1970s TV show. Maybe it was. *Who is responsible for the décor in this place? Mom and I could give it a major facelift.* There went my brain again, on one of those seconds-long breaks, to remove myself from the reality of where I was. Thinking about the terrible interior design was far more calming than thinking about this fucked-up situation. While we waited in an adjacent hallway with a few chairs, I couldn't decide whether to sit or stand, so I alternated between both. While standing, I paced back and forth in front of the chairs. *What if the grand jury doesn't believe me like the Detective Dickheads didn't? What if I draw a blank and can't remember a key detail from that night? What if I start crying on the stand? What if Shithead doesn't get indicted? What if I tell a different story from Boyfriend? What if I tell a different story from Cuz?* All the what-ifs floated around in my mind. *But seriously, who decorated this place?*

I returned to reality every so often and tuned in to the nearby conversations. Detective Z told us a little bit about herself. She was actually about to retire, and my case was going to be her last. Man was I lucky. She told us about some of her crazier cases over the years, one of which involved a rape case ten years in the making—a similar case to mine in that Detective Z had to make the phone call to reveal they had identified the rapist. Biggest difference was that this phone call took place almost ten years after the rape. Holy hell! I was suddenly thankful for my year-and-a-half wait, as twisted as it was. That would have been like me receiving a call today, in 2019, about my rape. Yeah, no thank you. The victim in that case decided not to pursue anything further. It made me sad to hear, but I totally understood.

Finally, it was time. A courtroom clerk called my name. I left the hideous hallway and walked by myself into yet another beige room with five rows of shallow stadium seating. There was a little chair behind a podium serving as the witness stand at the front of the room, just as you would see in a trial courtroom. The clerk motioned me to sit in it. I kept my head lowered upon entering and didn't look up until I sat down. I stared at my hands for a second. Jesus, I was sweaty, and not only on my hands. My neck was dripping underneath my hair, the backs of my knees were soaked, and when I crossed my legs, one thigh almost slipped off the other. Then I felt some drips on my belly—I had some legitimate under-boob sweat going on. How lovely. I slowly raised my head to scan the room. All these people were staring at me, probably noticing the immense amounts of sweat.

I sat for a few moments while Attorney got organized. Naturally, this allowed me one of those two-second breaks from reality. I made eye contact with a few folks. I wondered what their lives were like and how they had gotten selected to be there that day. Most everyone was middle-aged, some significantly older, maybe a few closer to my age. For the most part, they were all normal-looking people who were about to get slapped in the face with my sordid tale. Did they know what type of case this was? Did they know about the DNA that had been taken off me? Probably not. I needed to make sure they all knew this was going to be an easy decision for them without directly telling them. Dear God, I *needed* it to be an easy decision for them.

Attorney began his questioning. The questions were open-ended and meant to allow me to tell my story. For example, "Please tell the jury about the night of June 28, 2008, and the morning that followed." My response consisted of the exact same story I had told Attorney months prior and the police on June 29, 2008. I never wavered. I noticed gasps, open mouths, slightly shaking heads, and wide eyes during the milliseconds of me making eye contact. The jury was taking this all in, and I think they believed me, but they reacted in sheer disbelief. It didn't make my sweating situation any better, but it relaxed me a smidge. I had never shared what happened to me to such a large group; it was always one person, maybe two. The further along I got into the events of that night, the more focused the grand jury's faces became. One of the parts of my story Attorney was particularly drawn to was how I knew what to do after I was raped. He wanted to make sure the grand jury heard that piece.

He proceeded, "Rachael, please tell us how you knew what to do after your attack." I cracked a small smile in Attorney's direction and told the jury about my fondness for Lifetime movies. A few people chuckled, which was a nice reprieve from the weight of everything I had just said. Everyone born before 1995 knows about Lifetime movies. They start off with some sort of happy scenario: man and woman fall in love; a girl gets the guy she has been pining after; a guy chases after the girl, and after much resistance, she caves. Then, shit hits the fan: husband has an affair; an ex-lover comes back to taunt a family; a man rapes a woman and leaves her for dead. There is usually a police component, a hospital stay, a courtroom with a trial or a hearing, and then the bad guy is caught. Cheesy, happy ending, all is done. It takes you on a two-hour roller coaster of emotions and that's it. But never fear; there is always another nail-biter coming up next.

The Lifetime bit was relatable, and it legitimately made a difference in what I did after the rape. Thanks, Lifetime. While the movies may be corny, they were mostly accurate, at least when it came to rapes.

I noticed after a while how red one of my fingers was. Without realizing, I was vigorously spinning one of my rings round and round, and it started to dig into my finger. *Ouch, that's going to hurt later.* Sweat and a swollen finger did not make a good combo. But if that was my only battle wound coming out of this, I'd take it.

Finally, I was at the end of my story. It seemed like I had been talking for three hours, but I think it was only about twenty minutes. Another interesting fact about a grand jury is that they can submit questions for an attorney to ask. I got two, only one of which I can recall. It asked how I was doing two years after. *Ha! Let's see, do they want to hear about drunken therapy or sober therapy?* I downplayed it a little, and explained that I was still struggling for sure, but I was motivated to have some closure, which was true. It was a very politically correct answer. Business school did teach me how to be wise with my wording, after all.

I answered the other question rather quickly, and, with that, I was free to go.

I rose from the chair, hoping to God I didn't have any embarrassing sweat stains. The seat was covered in my butt sweat, evidenced by the wet imprint I saw when I stood up. *Gross.* I focused hard on getting down from the witness stand. *Don't fall . . . put one foot in front of the other . . . just don't fall.* My feet were so sweaty they could have easily slipped right out of my black pumps. I was shaky, and my heart was beating out of my chest. I didn't realize how tense my body was while sitting up there until I started walking.

Phew, out of the room. My focus shifted to how I did on the witness stand. *Did I convince them? Did I leave anything out? Should I have gotten more questions?* Nothing I could really do about it now. I gave it my best.

Anytime you go through something that consumes so much of your energy, it takes a while to come down off that high. I was drained but felt like I could run to the White House and back. My mind was spinning and adrenaline-charged, but my body felt like a noodle. Stress is so weird. It can have an intense physical effect without you even realizing it. *What am I going to do with myself now?* I took the day off work, obviously. I had already used my brain enough. *How about some lunch?* Yeah, lunch sounded good.

Chapter 26
Back to NC, Whoopee!

In the days following the grand jury, Attorney let me know how sympathetic the jury was and how badly they felt for me. All the witnesses did a wonderful job, and he was hopeful. A few weeks later, we got the news that Shithead was indicted, and my case was most likely going to trial. HELL YES. It must have been the Lifetime connection. I was so relieved that it all wasn't for nothing. Had he not been indicted, that probably would have been the end of the road.

Now that he was indicted, I could learn his name, right? Wrong. Shithead was still nameless and would remain that way for a few more months. I wasn't quite sure what the next step was; however, I expected radio silence because that was how it usually went, especially after a major development. It was like everyone in the justice system had to take a breather and gather themselves. I know, I know, my case wasn't the only one, and these people worked their asses off. But a few communication improvements wouldn't hurt.

Thankfully, the indictment news was followed by equally good—if not better—news. My work transfer to the Raleigh office had officially been approved, and I was getting the hell out of Virginia.

Eight months in the making, my firm had agreed to let me work remotely for my DC client through year-end, and I could live in Raleigh. I was finally going home. After the grand jury, I survived yet another busy season, as we had to file all the tax returns that were extended during the spring busy season, and I geared up to ship out mid-September. There would be no more long-distance relationship, no more long, dreadful commutes to my office, no more cabs, no more metro, no more overly expensive apartment, and no more DC triggers. I was going to be free from this place. It was like Christmas.

Arriving back in North Carolina, I rented a cute little one-bedroom apartment about a mile from D's apartment. We decided we shouldn't live together right off the bat. I had made that monumental mistake before. *Mistake* is a bit harsh. *Unfortunate experience* that didn't pan out the way I thought it would is more like it. We wanted to live together before marriage—yes, we had briefly discussed the possibility of marriage (whoa!)—just not right away. This was a smart idea. My Raleigh apartment was perfection. My mom and I decorated it pretty much the same as my Virginia apartment, and painted the walls Sherwin Williams "Hamilton Blue" in the living room and "Grape Leaves" green in my bedroom. I love the names of paint colors. I would never do it today, but in 2010, I adorned my new apartment in total *HGTV* style. The floor plan was very open with a huge living room, tiny kitchen, good-sized bedroom, and a small hallway to the bathroom. There was a cute little desk nook area, which fed my desire for extreme organization. And, most importantly, it had an alarm key pad right next to the door. I could set up a code through the apartment complex for no additional charge, and it would sound if someone broke in. It wasn't connected to the police, but it was a loud-ass alarm, so it would have scared the bejesus out of anyone. It was literally the perfect little place. Freedom! It was all mine, but more importantly, it was not in Virginia. That was crucial.

Being back home felt amazing. It's crazy what can happen in a year. I was back in my element with D, my family and friends. Everything was familiar. I never realized how much I could miss a Target, and a Starbucks where the baristas used to know my name. Basically, I was never leaving Raleigh ever again.

Chapter 27
The Second Layer

I needed to know Shithead's name. I fixated on it every day. He needed to become a person I could officially blame for raping me. I had a vague, fuzzy memory of what he looked like, as it was dark, after all. Picturing his face was difficult. I desperately needed to know his name.

It had been about nine months since my rape kit had been tested, and the authorities knew who Shithead was, yet his victim did not. There was something inherently wrong with that. I understand not releasing this information to the public, but *I* wasn't the public. I was the fucking *star witness* in the case. I had already been made to feel like a statistic several times over, and then some more. It was the least they could do. Of course, it wouldn't happen until the authorities were ready.

My mom and I decided to do some investigating of our own. We weren't going to sit there and do nothing. It was not in our nature. On one of the official-looking court papers I had been given, there was a six-digit number that piqued our interest. Maybe it could be my case number? Shithead was officially indicted in the District of Columbia on November 11, 2010, so we had a date, and we had a number. We gave it a whirl. Our first attempt was through the criminal docket website for the District. You can search cases if you have the right information, which we were hopeful we did.

Our six-digit number didn't work. Never fear, there was an email address, and my mother always taught me that there was absolutely no harm in asking. My mom ended up sending the email, as it was all a bit nerve-wracking for me—not that it wasn't for her, but she took one for the team. The subject line read, "Cannot find docket/indictment record," precise and to the point. Her email read:

> Hello—I'm trying to look at the docket for a case that was processed on November 11, 2010. This is an indictment for sexual assault and kidnapping, filed by the US Attorney's office. My daughter was the victim and the crime occurred on June 29, 2008. She has given me a possible case number (XXXXXX) but I can't seem to find the record. I'm not sure if I'm putting in the correct Case Type. Any help you could provide would be appreciated.

We figured it was a long shot and that our email wasn't going to an actual person. Rather, it would go to one of those generic email dumps that sends back an automatic reply thanking us for contacting them while politely letting us know we would receive a response shortly, blah blah blah. Fat chance. To our surprise, we received a response the very next day. It was from a real person, a lady to be more specific. How about that? Something went our way for once, probably because we were doing it on our own. Go figure. Her response was as follows:

> The number you provided is not a valid case number for the Superior Court of the District of Columbia. In order to look up the case number you will need the defendant's name and if it is a common name, the date of birth. I hope this has been helpful. Thank you for contacting the Superior Court of the District of Columbia.

Damn. We tried. We were going to need Shithead's name; there was no way around it. My mom, being the great mother she was, had no intention of giving up that easily. She asked me if she could call Attorney.

She didn't want to overstep, and I really appreciated that. I assured her she could absolutely call Attorney. Since he was so adamant about not giving us a name, perhaps he would give up the case number so we could find the name on our own. He wouldn't have to tell us anything he didn't want to, yet we would have what we needed for the criminal docket website. Sounded like a win-win, and I was all for a win. She called and explained that Shithead being in prison was public information, so I should have a right to know who he was, right?

Wrong. He still wouldn't give her the name. *Seriously? What the hell?*

Regarding my job—because, oh right, I had one of those, even though it felt like my part-time gig on top of all my case shit—I began working at my firm's downtown Raleigh office while I still serviced my DC client. Technically I could have worked from my apartment, but I figured I should meet a few folks I'd work with come the New Year. It was a significantly less modern office than where I came from. It had those high-walled cubicles; you couldn't tell who else was in the office because they were more like little rooms. Nobody knew me from Adam, so I could come in, do my work, and leave. No need to put on Face, because I didn't really talk to anyone. I met some folks in the tax department, but it was incredibly small. I now understood why they weren't taking campus hires a year earlier.

The Tuesday before Thanksgiving, I happened to be in the office wrapping some things up before the holiday. In my groove, casually sitting in my cubicle, I received a phone call. Of course, always when I least expected it, I looked down at my phone and Attorney's name was glaring back at me. *Oh Lord, what now?*

The onion was about to come back into the picture, the second layer's peeling producing a more pungent odor than the first. My case was officially going to trial. Shithead and his terrible lawyers decided not to take a plea. A plea bargain always sounded like a lighter punishment to me, but that is not always the case. Offering a plea is a way to reach an agreement so that the parties involved can avoid a trial. Not sure what type of plea Shithead was presented with, but the idiot wasn't interested.

The next reason for Attorney's phone call was the most important: He FINALLY revealed Shithead's real name. Holy shit, I had it! Holy shit.

My mom's phone call to him clearly made a difference. Attorney told me not to broadcast this information because technically I still shouldn't know—no clue why, maybe something to do with the impending trial. He trusted that I wouldn't go interview with the press, so he told me.

I didn't even care about the trial. I had the name. Shithead finally became a person. I felt the tears welling up; I had just peeled the second layer of the onion, and the deeper you go, the more crying there is. At that moment, I was thankful for my high-walled cubicle. I didn't want anyone to see or hear me, especially since no one in the office was a knower yet. I thanked Attorney profusely, and, after getting off the phone, I couldn't focus on work. I immediately called my mom and D and told them the news. We were excited and also petrified at how real the case suddenly became. I then decided it was time the Raleigh office needed a knower.

The tax partner's office was a few feet away from where I sat. Jittery and wiping the few tears away from my face, I ventured to her office. Since it was two days before Turkey Day, hardly anyone was in the office, but thankfully she was. I knocked on her door and timidly asked if she had a minute. I had met her a few times, and she seemed very personable and nice. She had approved my remote working situation, so I was eternally grateful, but she didn't know all the baggage that came with me. She welcomed me in, and off I went with the typical verbal vomit that usually happened when I shared my story: *While interning in DC, went out drinking, raped at knifepoint, horrible experience with the police, rape kit, grad school, moved back to DC to start job, case blew back open, moved back to Raleigh, and I just learned Shithead's name . . . a few minutes ago.*

I always had a *seriously, what the fuck?* moment when I said it all out loud, as I'm sure the partner did, too. She looked at me with sorrow and shock, but staying professional, she said she was deeply sorry for everything I had gone through, and whatever I needed, I should just let her know. Wow, she was incredible! For having only recently met me, an associate who had been with the firm for less than a year and was waiting for a spot to open in Raleigh, she did me a solid. I told her I needed to go home for the day, and her response was: "Absolutely. You don't need to be here. It is a holiday week, after all. Please, go home and take the time you need to digest all of this." Just the knower I needed. I thanked her, cried, hugged her, and left.

Chapter 28
Shithead Has a Name . . . and a Face

I became consumed with Shithead's real name. For almost two and a half years, he was a blurred piece of garbage engraved in my memory. Now, he was a piece of garbage with a name. It was a weird feeling. He was real and not just this figment of my imagination or the boogeyman in my nightmares. He was a human—well, I won't give him that much credit. He had a name, and that meant I was one layer closer to the core of that onion.

He had one of those names that half of America had. Whatever happened to originality when naming your kids? It wasn't like Maximus or Axel. Or even slightly obscure, like Bernard. No, it was one of the most common names in the world. Nothing about this ordeal had been easy up to this point, so why would I expect to easily find a picture of him? Silly me. My Google searches came up with odd and useless results. Some guy back in the 1800s shared Shithead's name, along with present-day doctors, lawyers, teachers, and even streets. I couldn't catch a damn break to save my life. Now that I had his name, I needed to see Shithead's face. Apparently, that was too much to ask.

Much like our first investigative round, Mom joined in on the facial search efforts. We went back to the basics. We knew he was in jail, which was revealed in onion layer number one. We knew he was in jail in Virginia. We knew there had to be record of him at a Virginia jail. We did not know my case number, and according to the District docket lady, if the defendant had a common name, we also needed a birthdate, which we did not have. We knew the DC docket website was not an option, and we stopped with the generic Google image and informational searches. We wised up and started searching through Virginia prison websites instead.

Never in my life would I have envisioned scrolling through prison websites, but there I was, typing Shithead's name into search bars, and getting no results. I even tried searches like Shithead the second (II) or third (III) and still got nothing. I tried typing physical characteristics of what I could remember: African American male, slender, tall. Nothing. I sifted through countless pictures of depressed-looking inmates. No luck. Personally, I would look depressed too if I were sitting in a concrete box all day. But that was the choice they made for themselves, so I felt zero sympathy for any of them.

The holidays rolled around, during which I took a search break to try and enjoy myself. Ha, enjoy myself? What was that like?

January arrived, and I still hadn't found a photo of Shithead. And of course, Attorney wasn't going to provide one. I technically still shouldn't have known his name at that point. On and on I went; a few months passed. I made it through my second dreadful busy season, this time in the Raleigh office, with tons of small clients who proved to be even more stressful than my one large one back in DC. Then, one random day in March, BINGO! Live and in color: Shithead. I finally found him on the Virginia police website. I immediately emailed my mom the link, to which she responded, "Fucking asshole stupid prick." How appropriate and concise. It summed up my feelings perfectly. My mom always did have a way with words.

I sat staring at Shithead's face. His mugshot eerily stared back at me through the computer. His head was slightly cocked to the right, and it was almost as if he had a crack of a smile on his face. Like a *damn, you've caught me* kind of look. He was wearing a red collared overshirt, probably with buttons down the front, with a white T-shirt underneath. The photo was low quality and cloudy, as I would expect for a mugshot photo.

It's not like it was taken with a Nikon. It's jail, for Christ's sake. They better not use Nikons. I recognized him immediately. Looking at him gave me the chills, and I instantly recalled the nightmare inside his car. He looked at me with those beady eyes, breathed on me with his abnormally huge nose, and whispered the words about killing me with his average-sized mouth. I hadn't realized how large his nose actually was until then. It was huge. Not sure how I missed that detail. Then again, I did have a knife to my neck and thought I was going to die, so I can't beat myself up too much over that minor, er, *large* detail. One of the more disturbing facts about Shithead was his age. He was forty-seven years old at the time of my attack. *GROSS*. I knew he was older, but not twenty-five years older. That was literally more years than my age. It made me a bit nauseated.

Along with his face and age, the website I found contained the holy grail of information. There were several fun facts about my rapist. He was six foot three (I knew he was tall), 170 pounds (I knew he was skinny), his eyes were brown, and his hair was black. There was a line next to his photo that read, "Violent: Yes." Duh. I'm glad there was no secret there. Further down the page, it mentioned that he was incarcerated for "forcible sodomy, rape, attempted forcible sodomy, and attempted abduction for immoral purpose clause II," whatever the hell clause II was. Fuck, that was quite the rap sheet. I didn't know yet what the charges were in my specific case, but this looked about right. I knew I was dealing with a major criminal, but to see it listed before me was a whole different ballgame. I had one of those *Twilight Zone* moments, with the *do-do-do-do do-do-do-do* music playing in the background. I had a lot of those moments over the past few years, like I had to pinch myself to make sure this was real.

Indeed it was. I had a pending federal case against a now forty-nine-year-old black male who was violent and already charged with rape and kidnapping. I was an almost twenty-five-year-old woman, victim, and witness in a fucking federal case. It was mind blowing, and really, *really* starting to take its toll.

Chapter 29
Side Story

Somewhere between learning Shithead's name and seeing his face, my mom and I learned of this story. I can't recall if Attorney slipped us the info or if we stumbled upon it ourselves, not that it matters. We knew there were three additional women who reported rapes against Shithead, and it turned out that one of them was involved in a lawsuit with a mainstream DC cab company. Well, wasn't that interesting? It wasn't the same cab company as the one I *thought* I was using that fateful night, but it was a cab company involved in another case, nonetheless. A woman was taking a cab home late at night about six months after my rape. Upon arriving at her apartment, in Alexandria oddly enough, the cab driver ran her credit card twice, only to discover it was declined both times. The woman was two bucks short of the fare, so the cabbie insisted he take her to an ATM so she could get the whopping two additional dollars to cover the ride.

The ATM was in an extremely dangerous part of town, and of course it was out of service when the woman tried to take out cash. As she explained this to the driver, he wasn't having it, and forced her out of the cab. Stranded, she began walking down the sidewalk in order to get to a safer location, and, as fate would have it, who comes strolling by? Shithead. He indicated he had a gun, and he would kill her if she didn't comply. He then proceeded to force her into a nearby parking garage, and brutally raped her. The woman survived, thank God, but according to the news, she was suing the cab company for five million dollars.

Learning of this atrocious story prompted my mom and me to do some further investigating again. It seemed all too convenient that Shithead crossed paths with this woman at 4 a.m. on a random sidewalk after she exited a cab. It seemed all too convenient that Shithead happened to drive up to me at 4 a.m. on a residential street in Washington, DC. My mom ended up requesting my phone records from that night from our cell phone company. As it showed, which we already knew, I did make two phone calls to a cab company. How did they not have a record of these on their end, as Detective Dickhead #1 had so nicely informed me? We concluded that, somehow, Shithead must have been intercepting cab calls. That was the only viable explanation that made sense to us. Unfortunately, we never confirmed that suspicion. To this day we still don't know, but it made us feel like we had at least solved something.

I also never learned the outcome of the other woman's case. But I would like to think she won every penny of that five million.

Chapter 30
Two Trains Collide

I was hitting my breaking point. Work was insanely busy, as it was now spring busy season once again. The invention of the laptop screwed the whole "when you leave the office, your work is done" mentality. People were now expected to be available all the time, any time of the day. If not by email on your laptop, never fear, you could be reached via email on your phone, too. Then, there was my second job: my case. Basically, If I wasn't working or thinking about work, I was dealing with or thinking about my case.

I was incredibly depressed, although Face did such a flawless job of hiding it that, except for a select few, no one ever really knew. That's one of the scary things about the varying levels of depression. I had this pristine outer shell, looked nice at work, and got my work done. It was a façade that drained me of any and all available energy. Once alone, I turned into this mindless blob that wanted to do absolutely nothing. The depression came in waves of severity since the rape, and this particular period was quite crippling. There were so many days I simply didn't want to get out of bed, but I had to. I had to keep going. Some days I felt okay, and I thought that maybe I was coming out of the dark days, but they were followed by even darker days. I looked forward to my couch, my bed, along with all the food in the world.

I was a depressive eater. I had always struggled with food and body image issues. No matter how many times someone told me I looked great, it didn't make one bit of difference. Food instantaneously made me feel better, but only temporarily. It was like my drug, except it was available all the time, and I could easily go to the store and buy it. Nighttime was the worst for my cravings. I'd be settled in for the evening, get a food craving, and actually leave my apartment (or send D) to go buy something sweet: ice cream, cookies, and brownie mix, which I would eat the raw dough and never bake into brownies. You name a sweet, I loved it, and I hated sharing my sweets. If I got a pint of Ben and Jerry's ice cream, the whole pint was mine. I would usually finish it in one sitting. I got a brief moment of pleasure from it, until it was gone and the sadness would set back in.

The guilt of eating whatever I just devoured, only to start all over again the next day, perpetuated the cycle of depression. I was sabotaging myself, I knew it, and I didn't care. Unsurprisingly, I began putting on weight, which in turn made me more depressed. The hot, skinny Rachael I worked so hard to become started to drift away. Then I would drink, which made it better temporarily, but the drinking would then lead to more bad eating. The vicious cycle continued like that for a while.

My depression had never hit like this before. I suffered bouts of depression when I was in high school, but nothing like this. It was debilitating, and I didn't really know what to do with myself. I lived in a constant state of worry and anxiousness. Anxiety and depression often come hand in hand, and I certainly fell victim to them both numerous times. I was worried about work, worried I would fail, worried I would do something to jeopardize my relationship with D, worried my case would never end, worried I was disappointing someone . . . I worried I was being too lazy, so I would hyper-focus on to-do-list items, but then I wouldn't give a shit and let things fall apart again. I worried about losing weight, but ate more to mask my worried feelings. I worried about making others around me happy. I worried my depression would shine through. That snowball effect was brutal. One minute I worried about running late for work, and the next I was getting fired from my job, and D was breaking up with me, leading me to a life spent alone. It was truly paralyzing.

I felt so trapped. It was like I was standing on the tracks, with two trains racing directly toward me. One train was work; the even faster train was the case. I saw them both coming, but I couldn't move. There was nowhere for me to go. There was no winning. At times, those scary thoughts of suicide would creep back in but then inevitably fade. I always reasoned myself out of it, but this was no way to live. These two fast-moving trains were right on track to a horrific collision, most likely resulting in some sort of mental breakdown.

Thankfully, at that point, I had a few knowers in my office, one of whom was my coach and friend. She provided me with not only work guidance but also life advice. She was wonderful and pivotal in preventing said mental breakdown. I explained to her that something had to give, and obviously the case wasn't going away, so that something would have to be work related.

She had never used it before, but there was a group within our accounting firm called the Leave Center. Come to find out, I could take a medical leave of absence and get short-term disability pay because of my mental health state. This was an extremely attractive option. I didn't want to screw my client teams by abandoning them high and dry, so I figured I could make it through the end of busy season, which would be Tax Day. Tax Day also happens to be my birthday. Funny, right? I'm the tax accountant who was born on Tax Day. I was set to go out on medical leave on April 15, 2011, making it the best birthday gift ever.

As this was a medical leave, I had to have valid proof that I was headed in the direction of a loony bin. Part of my sweet deal with the US attorney general's office was that I was assigned a victim advocate, like the one I had when I went to the hospital *that* day, but in a different capacity. This victim advocate was there to help me through anything while my case was ongoing. One of the perks that came along with having a pending federal case was this program called the Crime Victims Compensation Program (CVCP). I was one of the lucky eligible participants of this program, as I was the "direct victim of a violent crime." Recipients can receive money toward several things, including medical expenses, therapy, lost wages, etc., as a result of the violent crime. Because I fit the criteria to a T, all I had to do to receive some dough was fill out the application for this program, and my victim advocate would take care of the rest.

It didn't take long for my case to be evaluated, and, voila, I was awarded $3,000. How about that? Three grand. That's the going rate for a violent rape? No offense to the CVCP or anything, because, yes, any money is better than no money, but what a slap in the face. I don't know that any dollar amount would have made a difference in my feelings, but it seemed incredibly systematic. I could hear some male decision-maker with a deep voice say, "Let's give the rape victims three thousand dollars and call it a day. Checked that off the list, now moving on to the next issue." Yet again, I was made to feel like a statistic, and now June 29, 2008, had a price tag on it.

I used the $3,000 toward therapy services, some in DC, but mostly in Raleigh. My Raleigh therapist was the best of the best. She was my third therapist post-rape, and the third time was definitely the charm. In fact, I still see her to this day—not frequently, but I have check-ins. When the two trains were headed toward one another, I was seeing her twice a week, and she agreed that I needed to go on medical leave. She was my medical saving grace, as her doctor's note was my ticket to twelve weeks off work, with the added bonus that it was 100 percent paid. The accounting firm may have worked me to the bone during busy season, but they took care of me from day one, and I will be forever thankful for that.

I set my sights on April 15, and even had pep in my step after many depressed days. I told my teams—most of them were not knowers—I was going out due to medical reasons. I fielded a few questions, nothing too crazy, except for one coworker. She was relentless and way too curious. "Well, are you okay? What's wrong with you? Are you coming back?" Jesus, talk about an invasion of privacy. People kill me sometimes. I would never blatantly ask someone such personal questions about the reasons for their medical leave; I would wonder, yes, but no questions would leave my mouth.

Looking back, I was elated to know I had a huge break on the horizon. It lightened my anxiety and helped lift my depression for sure.

I remember thinking, *Three and a half months where I can sleep in, go to the pool, lay around all damn day if I want to.* It was one of the few times during those years I looked forward to something and felt some relief. What I didn't know was those three and a half months were not going to be as relaxing as I had envisioned. Nope, not at all.

Chapter 31
The Minion

Life is funny. You think and you hope that something goes one way, and yet often it goes in the polar opposite direction. April 15th finally arrived, and it was time for my extended break from work. My friends threw me a fabulous birthday/work-hiatus party, and I was thrilled to take a breather and chill. Turns out, I got a whopping ten days of chill. Ten fucking days.-

It was a Monday, and I had decided to stay at my cute little apartment that night. Usually I would go to D's or he would come to mine. But that night, I decided to lie on the couch and do my best impersonation of a vegetable: not move. Sounds nice and relaxing, right? I could not have been more wrong.

I had just finished eating dinner around 7 p.m. when I got a knock on my door. *Who the hell is that?* I squinted through my peephole in the door, and there was a guy standing there whom I didn't recognize. I figured he was trying to sell me something. *Cutco knives, maybe? Is that still a thing?* Perhaps he had the wrong apartment. *Maybe he's going to see his girlfriend or boyfriend? Or maybe he's a Jehovah's Witness looking to find new followers?* I didn't answer and didn't make a sound, hoping he would realize I didn't want any knives and that I was absolutely not his girlfriend. But no, he knocked again.

Dammit, come on, dude. He was ruining my introverted evening. I looked through the peephole again, decided that he didn't look like a serial killer, and reluctantly opened the door.

The guy looking back at me was a young-looking, short, geeky, glasses-wearing guy. He had a lanyard around his neck. He was even dweebier than high school D. He had to be some sort of salesman, and he appeared desperate to make a sale. I begrudgingly muttered a hello, with the intent of making this a quick "not interested and shut the door" interaction. He responded with, "Hi, I'm Minion (my name for him), and I'm with the defense team representing Shithead."

I'm pretty sure all the color in my face disappeared, and I instantly began to sweat. I felt faint, as my heartrate exponentially sped up. *Don't pass out.* I got that ringing sound in my ears, similar to when I received that initial phone call from Detective Z.

"I'm sorry, you are what?" I stammered.

Minion replied, "Um, yes, I am with Shithead's defense team, and I wanted to ask you a few questions about what happened to you a few years ago."

Oh, okay, so I did hear him correctly. He wanted to talk about what *happened to me* a few years ago—not what Shithead *did to me*, but what *happened to me*, like I slipped on a wet sidewalk and broke my arm.

My immediate response was, "You drove all the way down here from Washington, DC? As in, drove five hours to come talk to me at my apartment in Raleigh, North Carolina?"

He responded with a timid, "Yes." That was followed by a monologue of bullshit about how he wasn't a bad guy and that it wasn't a bad idea for me to talk to him. Oh, that made it all better. Phew, he wasn't a bad guy! No, he wasn't a bad guy at all! Innocently driving down to a victim's home for a quick chat. Hell, he probably wanted to come in for a nice cup of tea. To his dismay, I wasn't going to let him inside, strategically positioning my body in the doorway so he couldn't so much as see my Hamilton-Blue living room.

I was taken aback—blown away, actually. I had temporarily eliminated one train, and now the other one flat out ran me over. I had no words but knew I had to get him to leave. I basically kept saying, "No, I am not going to talk to you. I don't have to talk to you," followed by more bullshit from him about it being okay for me to speak with him. How dumb did he think I was? And how the fuck did he sleep at night, knowing he was representing the biggest piece of shit to walk this earth? Fuck him. Fuck him for ruining my relaxing evening. Fuck him for defending Shithead. Fuck him for thinking that my story wouldn't be the same as the one he already knew. Fuck him for thinking he could trip me up. Fuck him for only giving me ten days of a break. And fuck him for all the crap following his little venture down to Raleigh.

Minion was a degenerate that probably just graduated from law school and couldn't get a job in a legitimate law firm, so he took the first one he got with the public defender's office. What a gig. He also could have easily said no. When asked, "Hey, could you drive down to Raleigh, North Carolina, to go visit this poor girl who was raped at knifepoint by our client almost three years ago?" did he not think that sounded terrible? "We know there is clear DNA evidence, so we are pretty much screwed, but please go question her anyway." Sounded freaking bogus to me. But he did it. Lawyers have to earn their keep, I guess. Hope he had fun explaining to his boss that the prosecution's star witness slammed a door in his face. Oh, justice system, how you continued to amaze me time and time again.

He finally got the hint that I wasn't going to say a word about the case when I said, "No, I'm not talking to you, for the fifth time. And even if I did, my story is the exact same as it was three years ago in my initial statement, so why don't you just go re-read that. Goodbye." And I slammed the door in Minion's face. Looking quite defeated, from what I could see out my peephole, he left.

What the hell had just happened? I mean, seriously. Since my case was going to trial, the defense had the right to gather evidence just as the prosecution did. Fair enough. What's not quite fair is that the defense had the right to contact witnesses, regardless of how they were involved in the case. I was a witness, but I was also the damn victim. Attorney let me know that I might receive an email or a phone call, but not a fucking house call. I was completely outraged, blindsided, and scared that he might come back, but at the same time, I was determined. This guy threw me for a major loop and made me want to crucify Shithead in court more than ever. This guy had gone too far.

After Minion left, I immediately called my mom and D. My mom said, "I'm coming over, and I'll put the fudge on." Fudge moments occurred frequently, especially when we had new bombs dropped on us. She and D rushed over just as I began to crumble into the fetal position on the floor and sob. After my brief meltdown, while the fudge was cooking, we called Attorney to let him know about the night's big event. Like us, he was flabbergasted and disgusted. He suspected a phone call or an email but never would have guessed one of Shithead's guys would come down to interview me in person. Attorney informed me that I did the right thing. I absolutely did not have to talk to Minion or anyone for that matter. But that wasn't the only thing he told me. *How much worse can it get?*

Apparently, the defense could contact my family members, friends, and neighbors—whomever they wanted—in order to learn more about a witness. How lovely. Attorney was on speaker, and my mom, D and I all looked at each other, thinking the exact same thing. My dad still didn't know. I kindly reminded Attorney of this fact. I asked if there was any way Minion could visit his house, already knowing the answer: a big fat yes. Especially with how unique my last name was, it wouldn't be hard to track down any of my family.

Great, just what I wanted to hear. It was bad enough the grand jury hearing forced my hand to tell Cuz. Now, I was being forced to tell my dad. It was either going to come from me or Minion, and I wasn't about to let Minion have that power over me. So now I had to drop a bombshell on my dad, three years in the making. Fuck.

Chapter 32
Dad

M y dad is a good guy. He's the type of dad you call to come help fix a broken window at your house, to rescue you on the side of the highway when your car breaks down, and for advice on buying a new one. He is very even-keeled and calm. I don't think I have ever heard him yell in my life. He is an avid runner who has run more than sixty marathons in his life. He has a very consistent schedule. Wakes up, goes for a run, works, meditates, enjoys dinner, and then tinkers in his home office doing random odds and ends. He enjoys sending my siblings and me articles on new technology, travel ideas, and new places opening up.

Yet, our relationship was not always the greatest. He was never mean, never had any ill-intent. He just wasn't around a whole lot when I was younger. When I reached the age where I could decide if I wanted to go to his house every other weekend or not, I opted not to. I didn't feel like myself when I was there, so I stopped going. As a result, our communication essentially stopped as well. It wasn't until college, and after some therapy, that we really picked our relationship back up again. We would do dinners and catch up a few times a month. It was nice. When the rape happened, I never got around to telling him. I didn't want to disrupt anything, I suppose. Until, that is, that random Monday night when Minion dropped by.

After my call with Attorney and half the pan of fudge later, I called my dad. No answer. I left him a rather upbeat message hoping he was doing well and oh, by the way, asking if we could meet in person so I could talk to him about something. He called me back within a half hour; he was a night owl. He usually called around 9 p.m. on holidays and birthdays, so it wasn't overly alarming when he received my phone call at 8:30 p.m. on a random Monday. It was still random for him, but it wasn't going to be for much longer. We decided he would come over after his work the next day.

I spent all day Tuesday pondering how my dad would respond. I was sick with worry that he was going to ask me the very question my cousin asked: "Why didn't you tell me right when it happened?" I didn't have an answer for him. I did have plans to eventually, I guess. I almost told him at my graduation ceremony from my master's program. I had worn a strapless black dress under my bright Carolina-blue gown, and he saw my Live Laugh Love female symbol tattoo on my back, which he didn't know I had. I brushed it off, explaining that I just really loved the quote and thought the symbol was cool because I minored in women's studies in college. My dad wasn't really one to push the envelope, so he said it was nice, and we moved on.

Now, here we were on this Tuesday after the not-so-random Monday. I spent the whole day not relaxing but rather working out in my head the different scenarios of how my dad might respond. I convinced myself it was not going to go well. Finally, I got a knock at the door, and this time, thankfully, it was someone I knew. It was time to drop the bomb on my poor dad.

He sat in the beige velvety recliner I bought when I moved back to Raleigh. My mom was there on my beige Rooms To Go couch. I sat on the floor, fidgeting with anything and everything—my nails, the carpet fibers, some fuzz I had on my socks. At first, there was small talk—how are things, the weather's been nice, yada yada yada—but then it fell silent, and I said, "So. Dad. I need to tell you something."

Instantly the waterworks started, followed by the verbal vomit of what happened on June 29, 2008. I mostly looked at the floor, but every so often, I would glance in my dad's direction. He was crying too. Quietly crying, but crying nonetheless. That may have been the first time I had ever seen my dad cry.

He reacted so much better than I could have imagined. He gave me a huge hug and immediately asked what he could do, how he could help. He told me how glad he was that I was okay, and how he was so shocked that this happened. But he never, not once, asked my most dreaded question. And therefore I didn't have to answer it. To say I was relieved was an understatement. It gave me a twinge of guilt for not telling him sooner. However, I couldn't live my life like that. I made a decision. It wasn't right or wrong. It just was. And now my dad knew, so I didn't have to feel like I was keeping this monumental secret from him anymore. *Take that, fucking Minion.* Minion might have made me lose control for a hot minute, but I quickly regained it. He never did go to anyone else's house in Raleigh. Perhaps he tried, but got his wits about him when he realized it was a crapshoot.

Chapter 33
More Shit

My trial was tentatively set for November 2011. I now had six months to mentally and physically prepare for it. Shithead had six or seven charges against him pertaining to my case. I can't recall them all, but I specifically remember kidnapping, rape, and rape with a deadly weapon being three of them. The charges had fancier legal verbiage, of course, but that was the general idea. He had fooled me into getting into his car: kidnapping. He had sex with me against my will: rape. He held a knife to my neck while having sex with me against my will: rape with a deadly weapon. I didn't, and still don't, understand why all those extravagant terms and phrases must be used in the court system. Just lay it out there in plain English, for God's sake. The public knows that lawyers are generally intelligent. No need to further make that point with terms no one understands.

Unfortunately, even after the Minion incident and telling my dad the rape saga, shit didn't stop happening. It was never-ending. A very close friend and confidant, who was a knower, did the unthinkable. As I have mentioned, I was extremely strategic in selecting my knowers, and up until that point, I had done an impeccable job. Everyone had stayed true to their word, abiding by my wishes of confidentiality. Everyone understood it was my story to tell, and I didn't want to tell the world at that time.

Sadly I made one lapse in judgment, which came to bite me in the ass. Hard. This person told a rather large number of people, all of whom we both knew, about the rape. Not sure what was said or how the listeners reacted, but they knew. As the trend was, I called my mom, crying, to let her know that, once again, another bomb had been dropped. Completely shocked, she responded, "Come over as soon as you can. I'll put the fudge on." By that point, it was our motto.

I won't say much more, as this friend and I moved on after a while, but it crushed me. I spent lots of therapy sessions recovering from that devastating betrayal. On top of everything else, this was yet another instance in which I lost control. And I shouldn't have. I spent an absurd amount of energy keeping the rape locked away. I determined who knew and when. It is what kept me sane, in a way, calling those shots. So, for someone to so easily unlock it, especially without my initial knowledge, was tough. But we live and we learn, and we grow stronger from the unexpected. That's exactly what I did.

Chapter 34
Somehow

My break from work was far from a break. Thank God I wasn't working during that time; it was scary to think what might've happened if that were so. I would have ended up taking a leave of absence anyway. When I returned to work that July, my therapist mandated that I only work twenty hours a week so I could ease back in rather than go back full steam ahead. Again, I was grateful to my accounting firm. The company continued to pay me 100 percent salary during this part-time stint, as this was still considered a portion of my medical leave. It was all my brain could handle, and I was paying attention to that.

Somehow, among the never-ending shit, D and I were still going strong and decided to move in together. I was wary, given my track record. But somehow I knew we would be all right. He had stuck with me thus far, making him a saint. We went through a brief transition following the move into our newly shared space. How hard could living together be when we practically spent every single night together anyway? Well, when you spend every night together at *one* of your places, there is the option to go back to your own space. Once you live together, all of your space, with the exception of maybe your own drawer in the bathroom or dresser, is shared. That was difficult for me, as it is for many. I liked my own space. It always looked exactly the same when I left it as it did when I returned. I could control it and know that nothing would change unless *I* decided to change it.

In a shared space, I had to give up some of that control—*some* being the operative word. I got to decorate. What color did I paint the living room? Hamilton Blue, of course. I spared D on the green bedroom. Grape Leaves green was going out anyway. The difficulty mainly lay in all the little stuff that you don't initially think about: dirty dishes in the sink, wet towels on the floor, how someone loads the dishwasher or doesn't wipe the counters, and which one of you is going to fold the laundry. Some things were a bit more of an issue, like having people over when the other just wanted to lie around on the couch. D had always lived with friends, and over those past few years, he lived with a close friend. They were two dudes living in a man cave with mostly bare walls and three things in the fridge, one of which was beer. No judgment at all, it was just a different way of living than my own.

We got used to all these adjustments over time. None of them were deal breakers; they simply required a transition period. We had some arguments along the way, but I slowly became accepting of our shared space. I feared here and there that what happened with Boyfriend would creep its way into the present day, but it didn't. My space became D's space, and I liked that. It felt normal in my world filled with the abnormal. It felt safe. It felt regular, for once.

We got into a new groove, and things with the case shockingly calmed down a bit. Feeling calm was a nice reprieve. The impending trial caused me some angst, as we were sitting tight until I needed to begin trial prep, but I mastered my feelings toward it the best I could. My twenty-hour workweeks were very manageable, which kept me somewhat sane. Would you look at me—my life sounded almost mundane. I loved it.

Labor Day weekend rolled around, and D and I had plans to stay in town and hang out all weekend. That Friday, he worked in the morning, and we decided to meet up for lunch and play a round of Putt-Putt. Yes, miniature golf, a place designed for wholesome family fun, but of course D found one with a full bar—smart business model, fun for all ages. So we ate lunch, played our golf, took some cheesy photos along the course, and had a few drinks. We then went back to our apartment to wash up to go out for dinner. As we entered our abode, D mentioned he forgot his phone in his car, so he ran back down to the parking lot.

Meanwhile, I putzed around the apartment, procrastinating getting ready. D came back with his phone and a book. He motioned me over to the couch so we could look at it together. He explained that he made this scrapbook of the two of us to show me how much he loved me and how happy he was that things had finally settled down. It was perfect. As I flipped through the pages, gawking at the photos, we took a trip down memory lane. I remember thinking how damn sweet this all was. D knew how much I loved crafting, and I was quite impressed at his novice scrapbooking skills. Coming up on the last few pages, I noticed a picture of D's nephew. What was he doing in the book? His name was written underneath: *Will*. Next was just a picture of me. *You*, the page read. Then there was a picture of both of us that read, *Marry*. And finally, the last page was just a picture of D and the word *Me?*

OH MY GOD, D was proposing! He had stealthily slinked off the couch onto the floor, just in time for me to reach the end. I looked at him as he was down on one knee, and he was holding one hell of a sparkler in his hand. Shaking, he verbally asked me to marry him, and I screamed, "YES!" Was this happening?! At first, I couldn't really believe it; I was in complete shock. Then, I was ecstatic! Then, I cried tears of joy. I put these emotions on repeat as I stared down at my new bling, which was a stunner. It had one big diamond rock in the center, while little diamonds adorned the band. It was quite the beauty, and it was all mine.

There were no dinner plans; that was the ploy to get me back to the apartment. And when D was supposedly working that morning, he was actually out to breakfast with my mom, asking her permission for my hand in marriage. Incredible. He pulled it off flawlessly and somehow kept it a major secret. Bestie didn't even know! We spent the next three hours calling everyone under the sun. It was the best day. I cherished that day, as the good days were few and far between. As fate would have it, there were more bad days to come. But in that moment, it was the best day.

Chapter 35
The Third Layer

The closer we got to the trial, the more anxious I became. It was like I was in this epic game of cat and mouse, but the mouse was always barely out of my reach. I ran around frantically searching for it but always came up empty. Was this ever going to end? I was set to travel back to DC for a few days for trial preparations, and I had no idea what the hell that entailed.

Attorney mentioned my drinking *that night* could be the defense's focal point. He predicted they would try to use that notion to discredit my version of events. Sounded familiar. *Did the defense talk with Detective Dickheads #1 and #2? Let's hope they didn't.* Not a very strong case, in my opinion. Yes, I was drinking, but I had never experienced a more sobering moment than when Shithead turned the car off and demanded I pull down my shirt. Furthermore, the DNA said it all. So, I guess it made sense they were going to try and play the drunk card. Go right ahead. I wished them the best of luck.

As was the common trend in my case, things never went as planned. About a month before the trial and shortly before my prep, I got a phone call from Attorney. *What in God's name could be up now?* These calls were becoming all too familiar. Unbeknownst to me, we were about to peel back that third layer of the infamous onion. I sobbed as another bomb exploded on me: Shithead was going to be tested for competency. *What the fuck?*

What does competency testing actually mean? According to the *Journal of the American Academy of Psychiatry and the Law*, when someone is tested for competency, it is to answer the question of whether a person is competent, i.e., of the right state of mind, to stand trial. My answer? Abso-fucking-lutely. The court's answer? If there are signs of incompetency, competency will be determined through further testing. The journal states:

> *The standard for competency to stand trial was established by the Supreme Court's decision in Dusky v. United States with a one-sentence formulation requiring that the defendant "has sufficient present ability to consult with his lawyer with a reasonable degree of rational understanding—and whether he has a rational as well as factual understanding of the proceedings against him." Rogers and Shuman provide a legal summary of Dusky's three prongs: a rational ability to consult one's own attorney, a factual understanding of the proceedings, and a rational understanding of the proceedings.*

Well, how peachy. It was brought to my attention that Shithead started making comments like "I'm not understanding what I am being charged with" and "I'm not sure what any of this means." The defense had hit the jackpot. Shithead's comments elicited doubt about his factual and rational understanding of the proceedings. Not that I knew for sure, but it sounded like he was being fed lines on how to weasel his way into a mental hospital. What a nice break that would be from prison. Of course, I had so many questions. And I needed some penuche fudge. Mom to the rescue.

Starting with the most obvious inquiry, how was he considered incompetent when he had already stood trial in Virginia and been found guilty not once, but twice? He was serving back-to-back life sentences, for Christ's sake! As our fabulous justice system would have it, each case is looked at individually with regard to judgments of competency. Just because he was already guilty in two cases did not make him guilty in mine. The District of Columbia and Virginia did things very differently. Such a crock of shit, but I don't make the rules. Now my rapist was going to get a nice little stay in a mental hospital in DC.

It took an act of Congress for Virginia to agree to let one of their incredibly dangerous, already convicted criminals out of their jurisdiction and into the hands of another jurisdiction to get tested for mental competency. There went that jurisdiction issue I knew and loved. Virginia eventually agreed, and off Shithead went to a facility right in the heart of our nation's capital.

In my journey of writing this memoir, I decided to call the mental hospital where Shithead spent some time, in order to get a better idea of his stay there. I didn't initially mention who I was or what his name was, as it has now been years since he was there. I asked some general questions surrounding the process. The nurse tech explained that defendants are court-ordered to spend time being evaluated at the hospital. There are groups of psychiatrists, psychologists, social workers, etc., working to determine the mental health of these potential criminals. They observe patients in their natural environment, and have them undergo competency screenings and other evaluations. Then the different groups of professionals convene to examine the evidence of the case and the defendant's history, and decide upon a competency ruling to present to the court.

After her brief explanation, she kindly asked why I was inquiring. I politely explained that I was the victim of a case years ago where the defendant was sent to her very hospital for competency testing. Her tone immediately changed, with her stating that competency decisions are not made lightly. It was not as if people just walked in and walked out in the same day. She then went on to say that perhaps I should Google the competency testing process. *Why thank you, kind nurse tech lady.*

The call abruptly came to an end, but I got what I needed, which was a better understanding of what went on in such places.

Google explains that competency screenings involve looking further into aspects of the defendant preparing for and going to trial. Furthermore, competency screenings endeavor to find answers to questions regarding the relationship the defendant has with their lawyer, the defendant's general understanding of how a trial works, and if the defendant shows remorse for what happened. Once the hospital reaches a medical decision, it submits a report of their findings to the court, and if the court disagrees, the hospital typically conducts more testing. If the court agrees, then the case moves on to the next step.

So, (1) a trial occurs if the defendant is deemed competent; (2) if the defendant is deemed incompetent, an attempt to restore competency can occur; and (3) if the defendant is incompetent and the victim doesn't want to restore competency, the case will be closed.

Thanks, Google. All of this information did not and still does not make me feel any better about the entire competency situation. To me, it was all bullshit. Shithead was competent enough to rape me. He was competent enough to obtain and use a weapon. He was competent enough to drive a car, fake a customer cab call, fake being lost. He was competent enough to pin me down, force my clothes off. He was competent enough to then drive me exactly where I needed to go. I mean, don't get me wrong, someone must be some kind of fucked up to do things like that, but it doesn't mean they are incompetent. It means they must pay for the fucked up things they did. But again, I don't make the rules—I was only a victim of them.

Chapter 36
The Fourth and Final Layer

The waiting game again. The trial didn't happen that November, and we were now in yet another new year—2012 would be a pivotal year in my life. It was the year I would get married and the year this horrific ordeal would come to a close. Shithead had been in the mental hospital for months. He was there for so many months that it royally pissed off the state of Virginia because, somewhere along the way, the District violated the terms of their competency testing agreement. This only prolonged the case, to no one's surprise.

Attorney only gave me the highlights, never the precise details, of what was going on. I always asked a million questions to see what I could obtain, and he did usually give me more information than he was supposed to. But never was it *everything*. This waiting game, out of all of them, was the worst. Shithead's fate was being decided, and my case was in the hands of a mental hospital and its so-called professionals. I pictured him in there, sleeping in a comfortable hospital bed as opposed to a prison cot. Eating hospital meals as opposed to prison slop. Interacting with hospital patients as opposed to convicts. Wearing a hospital gown as opposed to an orange jumpsuit. Perhaps his hospital stay wasn't the way I envisioned, but it surely was not prison.

And then the day came. It was a day in May. A day when it wasn't too humid, the flowers were blooming, the sky was a gorgeous shade of blue. It was yet another day that began with such potential, only to be destroyed by a phone call. That day, it was the phone call conveying the decision that would change my life as I knew it yet again. The fourth and final layer: Shithead was deemed incompetent to stand trial for my rape.

Attorney said those words, and I had to ask him to repeat himself because I'm positive I blacked out. *Incompetent.* I'm sorry, one more time. *Incompetent.* Yes, I heard him correctly the third time.

After all that. The waiting, the phone calls, the grand jury, more waiting, Minion, the pending trial prep, more waiting. After all of that, he was fucking deemed incompetent. It was almost laughable. I had spent the previous four years longing for the day I would see this asshole in court and plead my case. And now there wasn't going to be a trial. I could not for the life of me wrap my brain around the fact that he was found competent for *two* cases in Virginia.

Apparently, the District of Columbia was a bit more lenient than Virginia with regard to competency, as Attorney informed me. That preposterous jurisdictional issue had come back around to punch me in the face. *Again.* I got the wrong side of the coin in the statistical flip. Just my luck. I did some digging on federal and state competency standards, and from what I read, Virginia had one of the more specific and lengthier policies. Some states barely had a paragraph describing what it took to determine competency. Virginia was not one of those; no wonder it got so infuriated with the District.

I was determined to have my day in court. I said from day one I would face Shithead again, no matter what. He would know who I really was. He would see my face in the daylight. And I would get to say to him whatever the hell I wanted. Attorney was incredibly sympathetic, and he promised he would do everything in his power to make my day in court happen. I was in a weird spot. I was relieved I wouldn't have to undergo cross-examination, yet I wanted justice. Most importantly, I wanted Shithead to know he wasn't getting away with what he did to me. May have taken years to nail his ass, but it was nailed.

Because he was declared incompetent, I was given the option to restore Shithead's competency. To restore, or not to restore, that was the question. It took me about two minutes to generate my answer. And it was a big fat FUCK NO.

This may come as a surprise, so let me explain my thoughts. First, he was a piece of shit who I wholeheartedly believed was feigning mental illness. Second, restoring competency would mean him spending even *more* time than he already had in the DC mental hospital—equating to even *less* time in prison. And I wanted him back in his Virginia cell. Third, the process could take years. YEARS. This aspect was the ultimate deciding factor for me. I needed to be done. The thought of this dragging on was absolutely daunting. I was so thankful the choice was up to me; it was one of the very few decisions I actually got to make. At least this was an important one. If Attorney could now make my day in court happen, I would be one happy victim. It all came down to that.

Chapter 37
Take That

A few weeks passed with no word of a potential court appearance. It was sickening how accustomed to the waiting we all had become. I was in the thick of planning for my wedding that fall, which I enjoyed for the most part. It took my mind off the case and was loaded with projects needing to be organized and coordinated, and I had complete control over it. We were getting married in a space resembling a warehouse, with old wooden beams and exposed metal staircases. It was a blank canvas, and my mom and I had our metaphorical paints and brushes ready to create a masterpiece. It was going to be my dream and would be even dreamier if my case were finally over.

On a fateful day, I received one of the last phone calls from Attorney, with *good* news for once. Praise the Lord. The final hearing was set, announcing we were not going to pursue competency restoration. Most importantly, I was given the green light to deliver a victim impact statement, despite this only being a hearing and not a trial. *Jackpot!* In a way, it was a complete win-win. I didn't have to take the stand. I didn't have to defend my actions from *that* night. I didn't have to go through being made to look like a drunken slut. I didn't have to relive anything in front of a trial jury. But I did get to face Shithead. I did get to speak. And I was hopeful to finally get some closure. The final hearing was set for June 15, 2012, exactly two weeks shy of the four-year mark.

A victim impact statement typically occurs at the sentencing hearing after a defendant has already been found guilty. Attorney went out of his way to make this happen; in fact, I would be setting a precedent in the

District by giving this statement at a non-sentencing hearing for a case with no trial. It was unheard of. But, dammit, it was happening. I had about two weeks to prepare for my day in court. The anticipation made me feel like I could poop my pants. I had no clue where to even begin but knew I had so much to say.

I wasn't sure if Attorney notified him, but I decided it would be a decent thing to let Boyfriend know of the final hearing. I sent him a quick and casual email. It read something like this: "Hey, hope you are doing well! By the way, Shithead was found incompetent to stand trial, so there is going to be a final hearing to put this thing to rest." He responded immediately, letting me know how strong I was and that it was completely up to me if I wanted him in the courtroom or not on June 15. I wasn't going to deny him the chance to fully close that chapter of his life. He would have done the same for me. We agreed that he should be there, and I was happy with that decision.

I gave myself two days prior to the hearing to complete my statement. There's nothing like waiting until the last minute. My mom and I were heading up to DC, and we decided to break up the drive with an overnight stay in a hotel. I was so damn antsy, so I decided to wander down to the hotel bar area and crank my statement out. I grabbed a pad of paper and a black pen and ventured down to the lobby. I found an open table in the back corner next to a window, so I had some decent light. I plopped down and stared at the blank, white paper. Scared thoughts crept into my brain, muddling what I wanted to say at the hearing. Maybe I couldn't do this. There was still time to back out. This was at my request, after all. I sat and stared for a few moments longer and then made a move.

Once the pen hit the paper, it didn't stop. The words came to me like magic. I could do this! I sounded sophisticated, pissed off, determined. I was direct and meaningful, sad and powerful. Not to toot my own horn, but it was badass. Sitting there at a random table in a random hotel, I felt this surge of energy. That feeling you get when you cross the finish line of a big race or walk out of your last final in college. That feeling like you could do anything and crush it. It was invigorating. Within an hour, seven beautifully written pages stared back at me. When I was done, I couldn't believe the words I wrote. It was exactly what I wanted to say, and I was proud of myself. I had come a long way. The excitement of knowing I would get to speak those words in front of Shithead, his defense team, and a judge was like no other. I felt all the emotions. I was nervous, giddy, excited, terrified, anxious, sad, mad, and happy all wrapped up in one. I never felt that way before, and probably would never feel that exact way ever again.

I wanted the courtroom to be stacked with knowers. My mom and D were at the top of the list. Boyfriend was coming, and to my pleasant surprise, so was my dad. D's parents were making the trip as well to show their support, which meant the world to me. No one, including me, had any idea what to expect.

My mom and I stayed at Cuz's house the night before the hearing. She and her husband were on their honeymoon; otherwise, Cuz would have been at the final hearing as well. (Side note: We had a very busy 2012. It was the year of weddings, ours included. I was in a few of them, and they weren't all local. We traveled to three different states, three weekends in a row. It was fun, but all of it happened alongside this final hearing preparation. Good distraction in hindsight. But holy shit, it was a lot.)

I didn't sleep well the night before. Who would? I tossed and turned and tossed some more. I stared at the clock; each minute felt like an hour. It was like the first day of a new school year or the night before a big trip. I tried counting sheep. That didn't work. My sheep were on crack. My mom once told me, "Try to think of nothing by forcing all the thoughts out of your head." Apparently that process puts you to sleep. Sounded clever, but again it didn't work. I had far too many thoughts to force out, and they didn't want to go anywhere. Once that seven o'clock hour struck, I was up and out.

It immediately hit me that I would be facing Shithead in a few hours. *God help me. Am I ready for this? Have I made the right decision? Do I really want this?* Yes. Yes, I did. I was as prepared as I possibly could be, and no one could take that day away from me. I tried on a few different outfits— knowing myself, I packed several. I landed on a dress. It was a simple dress with a white top and a slate-gray bottom joined by a black elastic band at the waistline. It was classy and conservative, and accentuated the thinnest part of my body. Despite it being a hundred degrees outside, I wore a black cardigan over the dress to hide my inevitable sweat stains. Hiding anxiety-induced sweat was more important to me than not being hot. I would be sweating either way, so I might as well attempt to cover it up. These were some of the crazy thoughts going through my head that morning.

I spent another fifteen minutes deciding on jewelry and shoes, finally going with some pearls and black pumps. I felt good about my outfit. I appeared well put together, though I was a ball of nerves.

Suddenly it was time to go. It had all come down to this day. My mom and I got in her car and began the drive to the courthouse in downtown DC. Everyone else was meeting us there. I cycled through emotions again on the car ride. *Am I really going through with this?* I thought I was going to hurl. Thankfully, I didn't, but it was a close call. Attorney had gifted us an exclusive courthouse parking pass, so we wouldn't have any issues finding a spot. We were like royalty. At least, that's what I pretended—royalty going to face a convicted rapist in a metal detector–equipped courthouse. A girl could dream.

We met D outside. Upon entering, we were immediately greeted by security guards who sternly instructed us to empty our pockets and walk through the metal detectors. It was like an airport on steroids. Then again, this was a courthouse, and I imagined there were some pretty shady characters coming and going on a daily basis. Once we got through, we climbed a wide staircase and ran into Boyfriend on our way to our designated room. We shared pleasantries, gave hugs, and he congratulated D and me on our engagement—it was only a little bit awkward. We were all adults and had moved on with our lives. Following our brief reunion, we made our way toward the courtroom, almost as if we were in slow motion. I wanted to go in, but I didn't. I wanted this to be over, but maybe I needed a few more days.

There was no turning back now. The doors to the courtroom stood two feet in front of me. Ultimately, I was ready. Or at least I *hoped* I was.

The courts run like sweatshops, cramming in as many hearings as possible in a day. There was no particular order; we were given a general time, and whoever was there and ready to go was next. I opened the oak wooden doors and walked in to see the courtroom was packed. Jesus, I hadn't expected that many people to be in there. I figured they were all people waiting to see other hearings. My crew of knowers sat on the front right side, while I sat in the second row between my mom and D. I death-gripped both of their hands, to the point where D had to let go momentarily because I was hurting him.

The courtroom looked like it did on crime shows but smaller than I envisioned. The judge was at her bench, and I was elated she was a she. There were two tables positioned in front of the sitting area, which had several wooden benches screwed into the floor. The décor was bland, much like the grand jury courthouse where everything was beige and wooden. I was cold but sweating, and was so nervous that my hands shook during handholding breaks. My dress's accentuating waistband was completely saturated. Thank God it was black. My armpits were drenched, too. I had flashbacks to the grand jury chair almost two years prior. *Wow, where does the time go?* Sitting and waiting, Attorney and the judge fiddled with papers, but nothing moved forward. One of my fears was that this final hearing wasn't going to actually happen. I needed this show to get on the road.

After a few more minutes, Attorney came over to our area and mentioned there was going to be a slight delay. *What the hell? What do you mean a slight delay?* The judge was going to hear another case before mine because they couldn't locate Shithead in the building! *Is this really happening? Is Shithead on the loose? Has he broken free?* We demanded to know what was going on. My mom sighed, rather loudly, and dropped her head to her knees. I sat there in shock, staring at Attorney. He assured us the hearing was going to happen that day, but he just didn't know when. *Is he fucking kidding me?* That was the cherry on top. Shockingly, however, the delay didn't last long.

Turns out, there was a slight miscommunication concerning where the courthouse was holding Shithead, so, for a brief period, the judge didn't know exactly where he was. He had not gotten loose out in the city, to my relief. In fact, he was being brought up to our courtroom at that very moment. We heard one of the doors open in the front left of the courtroom, and my heart skipped a beat. That familiar ringing sound flooded my ears. The room was still, and everyone around me was a blur in my peripherals.

I focused on the doorway, and there he was, slowly entering. There were some gasps across the room, including one from me. Shithead was in a head-to-toe orange jumpsuit, just as you see in the movies. Having never seen a hardened criminal in real life, I couldn't take my eyes off him. His hands were cuffed in the front, his feet bound with shackles. Four huge US marshals carried heavy, long metal chains that were attached to Shithead's handcuffs. Holy shit, these dudes were *massive*. Shithead had no chance of escaping them. He had no expression on his face. He looked lifeless. Good.

It was quite the grand entrance. The room went silent, and all you could hear were the clangs of the chains. It's a sound I will never forget. My mom doubled over again and immediately began quietly crying. It took her a minute before she could look at him. I was now profusely sweating and doing everything in my power to maintain my composure. It seemed like it took him an hour to get behind his table. Shithead's posse of three attorneys shuffled in past him, sitting on his right. It was quite crowded on that side of the room—eight people in total squeezed behind the small table. I bet they were all sweating too, as they should have been.

The judge addressed the courtroom, announcing that she would be presiding over the final hearing of *United States v. Shithead*. It sounded very official. I had one of those out-of-body experiences, where suddenly I didn't feel like this was real. Attorney snapped me back to reality quickly, as he motioned that it was time for me to speak. *Focus*. The judge proceeded by saying, "Rachael Ostrowski, the victim in this case, is now going to give a statement." Showtime.

Chapter 38
The Statement (Heard 'Round the World)

Shakily, I made my way to the podium, focusing on putting one foot in front of the other. I walked through a low wooden gate to get from the seating area to the podium. It looked like a little gate that grandparents would have in their backyard, leading to a garden full of luscious flowers and some tomatoes perhaps. Nice thought. And then, all of a sudden, my feet stopped, and I was about five feet from Shithead. *Breathe. Focus. Breathe again.* I smoothed out my papers, the words bouncing back and forth between looking blurry and visible. I took a deep breath, held my tears back, and started to speak. This is what I said:

"My name is Rachael Ostrowski. Today I have come to speak to my attacker and to our justice system. On the early morning of June 29, 2008, my whole world was turned upside down. I saw my life flash before my eyes and—in an instant—I thought this was it for me, at the age of twenty-two. And to think it was all because of this man sitting here with us today, Shithead [I said his actual name in the courtroom]. You were a complete stranger to me until that night, when you picked me up in your car, pulled out your knife, and did the absolute unthinkable. I have since come to know you quite well, not by choice, but through my nightmares, my flashbacks, and my deepest, darkest thoughts. What I have come to know is that you are worthless, a waste of life, and you deserve to rot in prison. I have waited four years for this day. The day that I get to meet you for the second time, and now that I am here, I have quite a bit to say. I used to wish that I had gotten a hold of your knife that night and did to you what you threatened to do to me. However, I'm glad I didn't. Because, this way, I will now get to haunt your thoughts and your darkest nights as you suffer in prison."

I had to take a brief break, as I got choked up from holding back my tears. As I paused to catch my breath, you could have heard a pin drop in that courtroom. I muffled an apology, and the judge simply said to take all the time I needed. I composed myself and continued.

"I can't even begin to tell you how you have affected my life for the past four years. You have taken so many things from me that I will never fully get back—my sense of control, true peace of mind and, mostly, my ability to see the good in people. I have had countless sleepless nights, hundreds of therapy sessions and have tortured myself with the events of that night, wondering all the what-ifs in the world that couldn't change the outcome.

"And yet, through all that, I feel sorry for you. It is your life ending, not mine. See, if you look around, I have the most incredible people in my life, who helped and comforted me through this horrible time. And on behalf of all of them and myself, I would actually like to thank you for not taking my life that night. Thank you for allowing me to succeed as a CPA, thank you for letting me live to meet the love of my life, get engaged, and later this year, get married. Over the years, I have had so many questions. What did you do the morning after you dropped me off? Did you go home to your family? Do you have a family? A wife? Kids? I wonder what they are like. How was your childhood? While I will never know the answers to these questions, the one conclusion I have come to is this: something had to have gone terribly wrong because how could you possibly have done this to me if everything had gone right?

"The reason we are here today is because this man, Shithead, has been declared incompetent. Well, no offense to the medical process, but I think that is a crock. To me, Shithead is completely competent. Well, the night I first met him, he was. Shithead, you knew exactly what you were doing when you picked me up, when you were pretending to talk to a customer on the phone, and when you said you were lost. And how about when you pulled the car over, swiftly climbed onto my side of the car? Pulled out your knife? How does an incompetent person do that? I just don't get it. I want to tell you and the court about my morning after you dropped me off. I went to the police station with all of your disgusting DNA on me. I was not believed and was made to feel like a complete statistic. I was then put in a squad car to be driven around to figure out where the hell you did this to me, followed by a stop at a freaking Starbucks so the head detective could get a latte and a muffin."

There were several gasps after the Starbucks comment, and I could see the judge's head fall in disappointment through my teary, blurred eyes. It once again occurred to me just how fucked up that whole situation was. I mean seriously. I continued.

"I mean, let's face it. I had all the odds stacked against me in what is typical of this type of crime. So why would they believe me? I was a white female crying rape by a complete stranger of the opposite race. And don't even get me started on jurisdiction. I was passed off from one to the next and, hell, if I'd known what a huge role it would play in all of this, I would have just said it took place in Virginia. The system should be able to handle this type of issue in a way that doesn't cause such detriment to the victim. And would you believe the detectives tried to tell me that this *would all blow over,* and *not to call my mom. It would be fine.* Unbelievable.

"Moving on from that day, the system just continued to shock me. It took a year and a half for my rape kit to turn up a match in the system. And that is considered short! And just when I thought the system couldn't disgust me anymore, I received a knock on my door on a Monday night last May. I thought, *Well this is weird.* I wasn't expecting any visitors. I looked through the peephole on my apartment door and didn't recognize the person. I thought it was a Jehovah's Witness and opened the door to say 'no thanks.' Well, I really wish it were a Jehovah's Witness, but, unfortunately, it wasn't. It was a member of the damn defense counsel who drove five hours down to Raleigh, North Carolina, to have a chat. *Are you serious?* First of all, if your client wasn't understanding you or the terms of a plea and was so-called incompetent, why go through the trouble of sending one of your peons down to talk? Were you thinking my story had changed? Were you thinking I would actually talk to you? Because, let me tell you. *Never* will my story change until the day I die, and never will I cooperate with anything or anyone who represents that low-life. Once again, I was completely revictimized. I would like to know how you all sleep at night."

That was the most exhilarating thing I said that day. Basically it was like a big *fuck you* to his lawyers and the justice system overall. Seriously, though, how did they sleep at night? They were heartless assholes working for what? To give everyone a fair chance? To feel like they were doing something good for society? People like Shithead didn't deserve a fair chance, and he was certainly not good for society. I still to this day don't know how his lawyers could defend someone like him. I would have taken one look at that case and said, "No thank you, next." I'm sure there are public defenders out there who are decent humans. But I have never met them.

I desperately tried to get Shithead to make eye contact with me. It didn't happen. He had his glazed-over, blank stare down pat. He must have practiced that during his vacation at the mental hospital.

"And after all this, no trial. My wish is that my statement today will open someone's eyes to how unjust our justice system actually is. And please know that this is not my last time speaking about Shithead and the court system. People will hear my story, and I will make a difference.

"To you, Shithead, I want to leave you with this: while this isn't a formal trial, I want to offer my 'recommendation' for your sentencing in my case:

I hereby sentence you to a lifetime of complete misery inside your concrete box. Don't dream. Don't wish. Don't have any hope.

Each night, I want you to see my face, hear my words, just as I have seen and heard yours for the past four years.

And, finally, if you ever have the opportunity to see life outside of your concrete hellhole, which I have been promised you will not, mark my word that my case will come back to haunt you, and that I will personally see to it that that *never* happens.

I hope you enjoy the rest of your life dying in jail. Always remember that I will happily be living mine on the outside for many years to come. Because, today, I am finally done with you."

Silence.

After the very necessary moment of silence, the judge commented how horrified she was that the justice system had failed me, plain and simple, and how sorry she was for everything I had been through. Not things I hadn't heard before, but it did hold some weight coming from a member of the court system. I nodded, cracked a small smile, and then glanced in Shithead's direction one last time before turning around and exiting the front area through the small wooden gate. The courtroom began clearing, and some of the folks seated on the left side shook my hand and thanked me for sharing my statement. Another woman remarked that my statement was the most powerful thing she had ever heard. I felt honored that it touched her in the way it did. Turns out, Attorney told several of his colleagues to come to the final hearing that day. Pretty much every person on the left side of the room was from the US attorney general's office. *Badass move, Attorney.* I loved it.

Leaving the courtroom, I felt a fifty-pound weight release off my chest. D held me tightly as I cried tears of relief that it was finally over. Four years of waiting, being blindsided, being betrayed, enduring innumerable anxiety-ridden days, and finally, *closure.* What a feeling! Shithead was escorted out of the courtroom in his clanging chains. What was a daunting sound an hour ago became blissful. Knowing that Shithead was officially heading back to his solitary confinement in a concrete hole was truly the cherry on top of my closure. My group of knowers plus Boyfriend all hugged me and told me how incredible I was.

On the ride home, Attorney called. Since my case was officially over, I guess all bets were off, and he could tell me anything now. He revealed that two of the other women Shithead raped were willing to testify in my trial, if it had come to that. I teared up, letting him know how amazing that was. Though it sickened me that the prosecution needed anything more than my story, corroborated by DNA evidence, those women will forever hold a special place in my heart. We didn't know each other, but we had a lot in common. We were strong. We were fighters. We were willing to stand up for each other. It ended up being a pretty great day. Closure was sweet.

Chapter 39
The Beginning of the Beginning

R ock bottom is a dark and scary place. I didn't really know what to
do with rock bottom, so it just kept getting deeper. After the final
hearing, I no longer existed at rock bottom. I slowly began stringing those
scattered beads back on the strand, the ones that flew off my necklace in
2008. I had found a few over the years. Beads of confidence, trust, and
love. The Face I perfected over the years faded into the background, and
I wasn't as scared to let my true self shine through.

I was about to get married. Talk about a bead I never thought I'd find.
The fact that I was not only able to begin and maintain a relationship, but
also have it be strong enough to survive everything, was nothing short of
remarkable. Relationships are hard enough as it is, and the good ones are
tough to come by. I honestly didn't know if a successful relationship was
in the cards for me. But it was. My knight in shining armor rescued me in
the heat of battle and stuck by me through the entire aftermath. We finally
got to a stable, beautiful place, in which we intended to stay for a while.

My wedding day was every bit of the little girl's dream come to life.
My bridesmaids and I spent the night before the wedding at my mom's
house. At about 5:30 the next morning, I sat up in bed next to my maid
of honor and shouted, "I'm getting married today!" We spent the day
getting ready at my mom's, with our hair and makeup ladies coming to
her house. It was the perfect morning: mimosas, hair done in the kitchen,

followed by makeup in the dining room, so much dancing, and all the special photos. I got the girls and my mom matching white button-down shirts with their monogrammed initials on the breast pocket, along with tall white socks to perfectly mimic the regalia of *Risky Business*. We all took turns throughout the morning running and sliding on the floor, paying homage to Tom Cruise. The champagne didn't stop flowing. Everyone helped me carefully get into my dress, and we all shared that breathtaking moment. I was a bride.

Planning the wedding served as a beautiful distraction, much like the beads and scrapbooking. I handcrafted the programs and menus, coordinating them with my overall wedding theme. I spent hours thinking about and creating the centerpieces and table settings. Tiny hairpins with faux diamonds at their tips speckled my updo. My nails were French manicured. My mom picked out my dress when we went shopping months prior. It was the second dress I tried on. She knew me so well. It had sparkles and ruching, was strapless and flowy, and had a hundred buttons down the back. I felt like a princess.

We rode in a limo to the venue, and I will never forget my walk down the aisle, in front of about 200 of our closest relatives and friends, toward D, with my mom on one side and my dad on the other. We were on the second floor of the warehouse. I glanced at the wonderland below and beamed, as it was exactly how I pictured it. D and I wrote our own vows, one of mine being that I would share with him my dessert, among several other sweet promises. That dessert vow is still a work in progress.

To this day, D says he didn't cry when he read his. But we both know he did. We took a thousand photos, and everyone enjoyed dinner. (D and I didn't actually eat until after the wedding; what they say is true—we were too busy visiting with people and completely forgot to eat!) Everyone danced the night away to the tunes of a live band. It was an amazing day—one of the best days of my entire life—and another step in the right direction.

Chapter 40
Speaking

Since my case had ended, I knew I wanted to speak about everything I went through. I wanted to make a difference, wanted to help others, wanted to do my part in stopping this vicious cycle. After some quick research, I found an amazing nonprofit organization in Raleigh that helped victims of sexual assault and domestic violence. It was exactly what I was looking for. I contacted them right away letting them know my interest, and before I knew it, I was registered for their volunteer training program the following January in 2013. I completed four intense Saturdays of training and felt ready to take on my mission. The organization asked me to speak at a large anti-violence event at a nearby college campus, and feeling invigorated, I jumped at the opportunity.

The event took place in a good-sized, open, outdoor theater. Numerous people attended, including one very special person whom I invited: my dad. He came to my very first speaking event, ever. Well, the first one not in a courtroom. Understandably, my mom was just not ready to relive it all, and I respected that. While I would have loved for her to be there, I never took it personally—she was always there for me, and I knew that. This was something I was doing for me, and she supported it, which was all I ever needed. When it came time for me to speak, the event host introduced me as a *rape survivor*. It was weird because I was historically described as a rape victim. Survivor had a nice ring to it.

I approached the podium. I was looking sharp wearing sleek black pants, a cute red top (it happened to be Valentine's Day), and a little black blazer. Not ready to speak from memory, I brought my notes up with me. It grew quiet, with only the sound of the breeze and the trees swaying. There were about 200 sets of eyeballs focused on me as I told my story from then to now. When I finished, people cheered and clapped, as I let them know that was my first public speaking experience. It was amazing! Someone gave me flowers, and my dad gave me a big bear hug. A reporter even briefly interviewed me for a spot on the news. So many other people came up to me, thanking me for sharing my story. It was my story and no one else's—not Shithead's, not the justice system's, not the police department's. It was mine. It was finally time for me to tell it, and it felt exhilarating.

Moments afterward, a woman approached me, and I could tell she was different from the others. She thanked me and had the glimmer of a tear in her eye. She then divulged an experience she had in college, over twenty years ago. A guy she knew raped her, and she never told anyone about it . . . until me. I was the first person she told. She was the reason I spoke and the reason I endured so much. She was my mission. To that woman, although I never did catch her name, thank you. Thank you for feeling comfortable enough to share with me. Thank you for being so strong. Thank you for giving me purpose. To that woman, I hope you are doing fabulous.

Working with this organization changed me. Every time I spoke, I healed a little. Since 2013, I have told my story on several occasions—at "Take Back the Night" college campus events, the organization's yearly fundraising luncheons, and on various panels. Some of my absolute favorite speaking engagements were the two times I got to speak to the Raleigh Police Department's newest officers, fresh out of the academy. They were bright-eyed and bushy-tailed, ready to hit the streets. That is, until they heard what I had to say, which was basically a "what not to do" tutorial on rape victims. They stared at me, petrified, and not one of them asked me any questions. Hopefully every single one of them listened and, at a minimum, never stopped at Starbucks with a victim in the car. One can hope.

After my first year of speaking, I was honored to receive the "Speaker's Bureau Volunteer of the Year" award. D and our large group of friends attended the picnic and award ceremony. They even made a congratulatory sign and held it up in the audience, chanting, "Speech, speech!" I gave a teary-eyed little blurb on how thankful I was to the organization and to everyone who supported me, emphasizing how much that past year had changed me. Afterward, we all went out for drinks to celebrate at a cute brunch spot close to downtown Raleigh. I wore a fun boho-style, flowy dress, and I actually felt pretty. It was a good day.

I am still a survivor speaker through the nonprofit today, primarily as the testimonial on the internal tours they do twice a month. To raise awareness, the organization takes small groups of interested folks through various parts of the building, explaining the services they offer.

One of those is a center entirely dedicated to sexual assault victims, which is where I tell my story at the end of the tour. Victims can come to one location and undergo their rape kit with a SANE nurse, meet with a detective, AND take a shower. When you first walk in, the lights are dim, the walls are painted a soft purple, and there is a sound machine playing the soothing sounds of a babbling brook or ocean waves crashing in the background. The front area has a few comfy couches and a chair with a small desk where the victim can complete paperwork. The center has an entire room with fresh, clean clothes for victims whose own clothes are needed by law enforcement as evidence. There are two examination rooms equipped with hospital-style beds, but they are also comforting and designed to look as non-hospital-like as possible.

The spa-like features of this center sure beat my experience of glaring lights in my eyes, having to walk past random people in the hospital waiting room, and sitting on a cold bench in a small room with white cinderblock walls. This center is one of the first of its kind. Hopefully, the trend will catch on. It's one of those bittersweet things. While it is amazing it exists, it is also terrible that it need exist in the first place.

This organization is near and dear to my heart and will be forever. I cherish my time spent sharing my story that continues to impact those who hear it. My mom attended her first event in 2018. It was the organization's annual fundraising luncheon, and it was at a gorgeous rustic venue in Raleigh. Purple and teal donned the tables—the colors symbolizing domestic violence and sexual assault. I was featured as a survivor in a video that was shown at the luncheon. I, along with two other survivors, was interviewed about my journey and how I got involved in the organization. I don't think there was a dry eye in the whole place, especially for my mom. I was so glad she came, and she told me afterward how good it was for her.

This organization has allowed me to see through a mission I never thought I'd have the opportunity to do: raise awareness through my story, and help victims of rape and sexual assault find peace and ultimately closure.

Chapter 41
Making Moves

N eedless to say, life had dealt me some unexpected cards. Actually, it was an entire deck of unexpected cards. I could have wallowed in that, and at times that's all I wanted to do. However, you don't get anywhere wallowing, so I chose to fight for this second chance. I chose to fight for a good life, fight to overcome the shitty cards I was dealt, and fight to string more beads back on my necklace. As hard as it was, that's precisely what I did.

The first move was getting the hell out of public accounting. This second chance of mine was not going to be spent working two busy seasons a year and never being able to turn off my brain. There were many perks to being married, one of which was the combined bank account. I ultimately decided tax accounting was not my thing at all, and, while the money was good, it wasn't worth it to me. I wanted to take a giant step back, focus on my speaking engagements and volunteering, but still have a job which I enjoyed every day. After many conversations and many job searches and a few interviews, I landed on the perfect job for me at the time. It happened to be at my same accounting firm, just in a different role. In a nutshell, I was going to be an administrative assistant, a MAJOR detour off the straight and narrow. But, hey, second chance life, right?

I didn't need my master's degree, didn't need my CPA license, and I didn't need the paycheck that came with it. I had to get over my ego for taking a "step down," which happened rather quickly. I realized I would never have known about this administrative position without my prior experience, and that's the way I looked at it. I took a substantial pay cut to increase my quality of life. A wise coworker told me that if you need to, take a pay cut earlier in your career, before you get comfortable living with more money. Didn't take much convincing. Money wasn't everything. Life balance was. We had just what we needed, and with minimal financial tweaks, D and I made it work. I loved my new job. I came in to the office and left at the same time each day, helped a wide range of folks with any internal issues they had, and felt deep accomplishment in the process. This job was yet another bead added back to my necklace.

People asked D and me throughout our first year of marriage, "So, how is the first year going?"—a question that carries with it the common assumption that year one is the hardest. My response was always, "It is truly great!" and I would get these extremely surprised looks followed by a "Wow! You must still be in the honeymoon phase—it will get harder." And I always wanted to respond, "Well, you don't know anything about what we endured before we got married."

If there is a hell, D and I had already traveled there and back a few times, making our first year of marriage a piece of cake. We lived together beforehand, faced a hardened criminal in court, planned a wedding, and didn't kill each other in the process. That had to count for something.

We bought a house, like married people tend to do. Talk about entering adulthood. No longer being able to call the maintenance man to change a light bulb was quite eye-opening. We had a yard. We now had to mow that yard. We had a real mailbox at the end of our driveway and didn't need a key to open it. We could park our cars in a garage and not get wet when it was raining. And all of our apartment furniture looked like dollhouse furniture placed in a castle. Our house was on a cul-de-sac and within walking distance to a bar. Jackpot. I went to town decorating, and made all my inner interior designer dreams come true. We refinished all the hardwood flooring downstairs and ripped up the builder-grade carpet, replacing it with a fun, shaggy textured one. We repainted in all new paint colors, by Sherwin Williams, of course—Plantation Brown,

Latte, Shaker Beige, and Gray Clouds, to name a few. Paint color names are so fun, much like Crayola crayon names. I wonder who thinks of them.

We made it our own. We were making some serious moves, and I loved it.

Now that we had our house, D and I took the bull by the horns and decided to really live it up. What better way to do that than to travel? D had never been out of the country until our honeymoon. Over roughly two years, we went to the Dominican Republic, Iceland, Mexico, Chicago, New York City, Belgium, Ireland, and England. The world was so beautiful. Escaping into other people's cultures was good for the soul and provided many perspectives. Occasionally, Shithead popped into my head, and I would smile. While I was staring into the night sky watching in awe the Icelandic northern lights, he was staring at a concrete wall. While I was napping in a cabana on a Dominican beach, he was lying on a prison cot with raggedy blankets. While D and I were enjoying the cast of *How I Met Your Mother* on *The David Letterman Show* in New York City, he was enjoying his toilet being two feet from his cot. And while we scarfed down hot dogs at the Cubs game in Chicago, he was eating prison slop. Now that was some perspective.

Chapter 42
Baby #1

M̲y second-chance life wasn't all rainbows and butterflies. Don't get me wrong, it was leaps and bounds better than it used to be. We were overall very happy and thankful for everything we had, but we still had our hurdles. Generally, when I decided to do something, I did it. And when I wanted something to happen, I wanted it to happen immediately. I always knew I wanted to be a mom. I wanted to get married, get a house, and have some babies. During the Shithead years, it was hard for me to take care of myself, let alone fathom the idea of taking care of a child, but the desire was still there. In 2014, that desire became a need. We desperately wanted to have a baby.

Month after month, all the tracking, all the sex, all the waiting . . . it started out exciting but quickly got old. My life revolved around that forty-eight-hour ovulation window, thinking we nailed it that month, only to be disappointed by a negative pregnancy test two weeks later. Of course, when you don't get something, it makes you want it even more. It felt like every woman I saw was pregnant and there were children everywhere I looked. Stores were stocked with maternity clothes and baby clothes and diapers. While these things always existed, I never noticed them until I yearned for them. The only silver lining each month was alcohol. Thankfully, Raging Rachael had retired for the most part, but I still loved my alcohol. I drank to have fun, not so much to black out.

We ended up seeking out a fertility specialist after trying to get pregnant for about a year. The doctor ran several tests, and, as it turned out, we had a case of unexplained infertility. It was such a devastating blow, and I was beyond stressed out about it all. So much so that I got shingles, the virus that lies dormant after chicken pox, which was a big neon sign with flashing lights that we needed to take a break and reevaluate. Stress is nothing to play around with. It was the eye-opener I needed to calm down and take care of myself. After a brief baby-making break, we formulated a plan, and I started taking fertility medications to increase our chances of conceiving. Round one commenced.

The waiting game was the worst, and I was all too familiar with waiting. The days felt like years, and with every little twinge, pang, and change in my body, I wondered if a baby was forming. *Is it time to test yet? Am I pregnant?* I had pretty much convinced myself I wasn't. D and I threw this huge engagement party for two of our good friends one weekend at the end of the summer of 2014. We had kegs flowing, a food truck, champagne, the whole nine yards. I had a blast, got incredibly drunk and then cried about not being pregnant. Damn alcohol always brought out the best in me.

The next morning, hungover as hell, it dawned on me that I was about two days late getting my period. With all the party planning, I got sidetracked from overanalyzing my fertility calendar. I decided that, since I was late, why not pee on some sticks. Bestie was with me, cheering me on. Five sticks later, they were all positive. I kept making Bestie look at them under a lamp to be sure. Oh my goodness, I was pregnant! Round one worked!

As luck would have it, Cuz, who also struggled with infertility, was also pregnant, and we ended up giving birth on the same day. Who would have thought that a couple of second cousins from different cities would not only meet on the same night a crazed psycho crossed my path, but would both end up living in Raleigh and delivering babies on the exact same day? Life is funny like that.

Being pregnant was all right. Not too bad, not too great, just all right. I could not wait to have the baby. I counted down the weeks and was always ahead of myself. We were elated to find out we were having a son—T, as I shall call him—a little boy to call me Mama, a little boy who was going to be ours. In mid-2015, after a hellacious labor and resulting C-section, I became the mama to a beautiful baby boy. What a life-changing day.

Becoming parents introduced us to a new level of chaos we weren't prepared for. Within the first twenty-four hours of coming home, we were peed on, shat on, puked on, and I was covered in milk. It wasn't anything like I expected. It wasn't calm or glamorous. To be honest, I hated it. But I pretended like I loved it. People would ask, "Oh, aren't you just loving it?" And I would look back at them with sadness in my eyes but respond, "Yes! It's wonderful," when really I felt ashamed, exhausted, and helpless. I was completely out of my element and had lost all sense of control, which meant only one thing: I was headed down a tunnel of doom once again. I mourned my old life, when I could leave the house whenever I wanted, take a nap whenever I wanted, and had a clear mind that made rash decisions. Where did all that go? In turn, I felt so guilty because I wanted this baby so badly. After three long months of never-ending crying and gloom, D realized something wasn't right.

Turned out, postpartum depression was a real bitch. We had heard the term once or twice but weren't fazed by it until it punched us in the face. Looking back, it wasn't surprising that it hit me so hard, as I had a mile-long history of depression and anxiety. After everything I had conquered and gotten through over the past few years, it was a harsh reality to grasp. Although it felt like a major setback at the time, it was all part of my process in this new phase of life. All my knowers rallied around me and provided incredible support. I worked with a psychiatrist who specialized in postpartum women; her calming and reassuring nature was just what I needed. She adjusted my meds and provided me with tips for surviving the newborn stage. I reverted to the broken puppet that needed to be moved and told what to do. Only, this time, I had a tiny human to take care of in addition to myself. Thankfully, our parents were at our beck and call, and they were complete godsends. With time, therapy, and loads of help, it slowly got better.

I started to love being a mom. The fact that D and I created this life was mind-blowing. T was a little cherub with red hair, blue eyes, fair skin, and a smile that could make the world melt away in the background. The three of us were a wonderful family unit, adjusting to our new life. As T was my parents' first grandchild, they went nuts. He was our prized possession and brought so much joy.

Returning to work was good for me after my maternity leave. I felt a great sense of self-worth and accomplishment, outside of being a full-time mom. It was nice to do something for me, which I didn't always do well. I think a lot of moms, victims, and people in general struggle with self-care. Not that going to work would necessarily be viewed as self-care, but it was for me at the time. It took about a year to really feel like myself again. I got back into exercising, eating healthy, socializing with our friends. The telltale sign that my old self was poking through, however, was the one-year birthday party we threw for our baby, who wouldn't remember a thing—it was really a party for D and me. We made it a whole year keeping a child alive, which was something to celebrate. We had a monster-themed party that was Pinterest perfect. There were squiggly eyeballs on everything, even edible ones on cookies, a monster smash cake, monster cupcakes, and a keg for the adults. Who doesn't have a keg at a one-year-old baby's birthday party? After a brief hiatus, I was finally back and stronger than ever. I was so strong that we decided to embark on the whole journey again two years later.

Chapter 43
Baby #2

I really believe that when mothers want another baby, it means they have completely forgotten what it was like to be pregnant and sleep deprived; at least I did. It all became a blur and distant memory. Our second time around was a bit more complicated as D was smack in the middle of an intense MBA program, still working full time, and we had an eighteen-month-old. The stress had taken its toll on D—not necessarily in his behavior, but on his body for sure. We figured we would get pregnant right away by doing exactly what we did the first time. After a visit to our fertility doctor, we had the meds, and got right to it. Three months went by, and no baby. I began spiraling down that dark hole of burning desire and desperation, longing for what was not happening. As fate would have it, our unexplained infertility had worsened, and we ultimately resorted to in vitro fertilization (IVF). One might think that was devastating news, and initially it was. But, to a planner, it meant there was a solution and, most importantly, a plan.

Going through IVF was brutal, but we powered through the shots, the hormones, and the discomfort. Both of us abstained from alcohol and maintained a healthy diet to give ourselves the best chance we could. We ended up with four perfect embryos, and, to our delight, the first transfer procedure worked. I got that magical word on the pee stick: Pregnant. We were at the beach with D's family, and while we said we weren't going to test until we got home, I couldn't wait. Shaking with excitement, I was so relieved T would soon become an older brother.

My second pregnancy was for the birds. I was so sick, so dehydrated, so uncomfortable, and suffered through countless migraines. I did decide to start writing this memoir while pregnant, so there was a silver lining. I also got to skip the hellacious labor and have a scheduled C-section. Our second precious baby boy, L, was born the same month as our first, in May, almost three years later. That moment in the hospital when your first-born meets the second-born is one for the books. Still reeling from the adrenaline of the birth, D and I cherished that moment, making it one we will never forget.

We were now a family of four. Going from one to two kids felt like going from one to twenty at first. How did people do this? I suffered another severe bout of postpartum depression, but luckily it didn't last nearly as long. Our second little redheaded joy, like his older brother, was not the greatest sleeper, but we plowed through it, and the sleepless beginning became another distant blur.

Our kiddos have given my life purpose, and I wouldn't trade the sleepless nights, the tantrums, the countless hugs and snuggles, the laughs, and the love for anything. It's something I am so grateful to experience. Our kids keep us on our toes, challenge us, push our buttons, and at times drive us crazy. But then our three-year-old calls D and me his *best friends*, and we instantaneously become mush balls again. We are raising them in a house full of love and laughter and also instilling in them the important building blocks of life: having respect for not only others, but for themselves; maintaining equality among genders, ages, and races; the importance of communication and knowing it is okay to talk about feelings; making good choices in good and bad situations; being kind to everyone and everything; and being honest and self-aware. As a mom *and* a rape survivor, it is important to me that my boys understand the severity of sexual violence and how they can help break the cycle. And hopefully by the time they have children of their own, our world will be a much safer place.

It's been a wild roller coaster of a ride so far, which brings us to where I am today.

Chapter 44
Phew

Wow, it's been quite the decade. Never in my wildest dreams would I have imagined my life going in the direction it did. I started out with this specific path because I thought that's what I *had* to do: get good grades in high school, go to college, get good grades in college, get a job, work my ass off, make money, meet a guy, get married, have some kids, become some big-wig partner in an accounting firm with a huge corner office overlooking some huge city. A lot of these things did happen. I got good grades, I graduated from college with two degrees, I got a job. I met a guy, I got married, I had two kids. But there was this major bump in my path: I was raped and almost killed, and when that happened, it set my life on a different path.

I didn't just meet a guy. I met *the* guy. I didn't just get married. I had *the* dream wedding. I don't just have some kids. I have *the* most amazing kids. They are truly the best, and I honestly don't know what D and I would do without them. I didn't do all of those things because I *had* to. I did them because I wanted to and, most importantly, because I could. For me. For D. For my kiddos. I am living the life I want to live. Life is too short to live any other way.

I started out in this very familiar world. It was a carefully selected, handcrafted, tightly beaded necklace. It then became very unfamiliar for a long time. Things got hazy, uncontrollable, scattered. The beads went fucking everywhere. When I started to put my necklace back together, it looked different. The beads were in a different order. I got some new ones. Some were cracked, others discolored. But the strand was the same. I am that strand, now just with a bunch of different beads. I am the same person, but also changed, for the better, and boy have I learned some things.

Chapter 45
Life Lesson #1

There are things I did not know at twenty-two years of age. There are things I did know but never should have known at twenty-two. Communication is my life lesson number one. Clearly, I communicated: I spoke words, and I talked to people, but that isn't the part of communication I am talking about (pun intended). It's not just about the words. It's about the type of words. Be honest. I think we tend to tread lightly with our words, so as to not ruffle any feathers or hurt any feelings. But we aren't doing anyone any favors. Being honest leaves nothing on the table. Say what everyone else is thinking. Push the envelope. Ever have that thought after a conversation, "Man, I wish I had said that," or "If only I had said that?" I have, plenty of times. I wished so badly that I had given Detective Dickheads a piece of my mind *that* day or even filed a complaint. It wasn't until years later that I built up the courage to call one of them. Say what's on your mind. You will never regret being honest. Well, sometimes you might, but you will always regret *not* being honest.

Ask for help. What's the worst that could happen? Someone says no? You will never know if you don't ask. We can't always do life by ourselves. It takes a village, and not just with kids. I have often felt I am a burden to others by asking for help. But the truth is, I become a greater burden by trying to do it all myself. I lose myself. I become exhausted. It's a lose-lose for everyone. Ask for help. Chances are someone will say yes every single time and not mind at all.

That saying "You never know what someone might be going through" became a saying for a reason: because we don't know. We don't communicate enough. People hide behind these faces and suffer. I did for years. Face was my survival. I'm not saying you must tell everyone what is happening in your world, but tell someone: a therapist, a friend, a family member, a neighbor, a spouse, a coworker. Someone. Everyone needs knowers. Without them, we won't make it.

That day, I was angry, I was hurt, and I felt betrayed. I showed the anger for sure, but I didn't verbalize the hurt and the feelings of betrayal. I never said the main reason I felt those emotions was because of how much I loved Boyfriend. We went our separate ways on the worst note, and when we came back together again, less than twenty-four hours later, everything was so messed up. I came close to never being able to communicate again. My point: tell the people you love that you love them. Pick up the phone, talk to your loved ones. See how they are doing. Do not just text or email or hide behind some other form of technology. Tell people you love them as much as you possibly can. Because, one day, you may not be able to and will wish that you had.

Communication is key. It is key in relationships, at work, with strangers, with your kids. But it takes a ton of practice. I am by no means perfect at communicating, but I have made major improvements over the past ten years. Silence was never going to be okay for me. Martin Luther King Jr. once said, "Our lives begin to end the day we become silent about things that matter." That couldn't be truer, even half a century later. My rape is an uncomfortable subject, but it doesn't have to be. For years, I couldn't even say the word *rape*. It was always "attack" or "that thing that happened in 2008." Why? Because it made people antsy, which would make me antsy and then ashamed.

Rape is a word, and it's the truth. I wasn't just attacked. It wasn't just a thing. It was rape. I can say that word now. It still makes me cringe a little, but I am not ashamed anymore. The word does not define me. I define it.

Chapter 46
Life Lesson #2

⌢•••••⌣

Love yourself. Be yourself. Stay true to yourself. Of all the things I know now, this is probably the most important one. After the rape, I felt worthless, stupid, and endlessly guilty. How could I have let that happen? I was extremely hard on myself and beat myself up for a very long time. Once I finally came to terms with the fact that the rape wasn't my fault, and I stopped blaming myself, I was able to start loving myself again.

I am a huge quote person. I love searching for them, I love thinking about them, and I love sharing them. They make me feel warm and fuzzy inside, and they are good for my soul. One of my particular favorites, of unknown origin, is this: "Be gentle with yourself. You're doing the best you can."

Cheesy as it may be, these words hold so much truth. Some days, you just need a break, a mental health day, time to regenerate. Allowing yourself the time to heal is so important. It is okay to *not* be okay. Recognize it, embrace it, and accept the season of life you are in. We will all go through some type of trauma or heartbreak or devastation in our lives, and you will be the one to ultimately bring yourself to the other side. Yes, there will be supporters and knowers and loved ones along the way, but *you* are the one who will get yourself there. You have to figure out how to cope and work your ass off in the process, but you will get there. You have to be gentle with yourself and allow yourself the time to do so. Loving yourself is hard. We are indeed our own biggest critics. Like most other things in life, it takes practice.

I have been in situations where I won't act a particular way because it might mean others won't like me. I still do it sometimes to this day. What the hell is up with that? Why do we do things like that? Not everyone is going to like you. I struggle with that, as I am the ultimate people pleaser. But in trying to stay true to myself, I have gotten better. It's much easier said than done to not give a shit what other people think, especially in this media-crazed day and age. Your body should look this way, you can't wear that, your face should always look airbrushed, blah blah blah. But if you can find ways to tune all of that out and focus on yourself, it will do wonders. At the end of the day, you have yourself. So cut yourself some slack and pour on some love.

Chapter 47
Life Lesson #3

Live every day like it could be your last. Cliché as all hell, I know. But I am now a firm believer that this is how life should go. Life happens, and there are things that must get done: mundane things like laundry, cooking, putting gas in your car, taking a daily shower, and more significant things like moving, dealing with getting laid off, mourning a death in the family. In the midst of all the noise, you can still do something every day, just for you, that you love and want to do.

After my second little miracle was born, I did something insane. Something I did not think I would ever do. Something people do all the time, but not me. I quit my job. I returned to the accounting firm for a whopping four days after my second maternity leave, and then put in my two weeks' notice. I left the straight and narrow. Not only did I quit my job, I decided to be a stay-at-home mom with L, while T stayed in preschool. Were pigs flying? Me, the type A college student turned rape victim turned accountant turned survivor was now a stay-at-home mom. My, how the tides had turned. I couldn't believe I actually pulled the trigger, but I did. I figured, *If I die tomorrow, would I die happy?* Yes, for a lot of reasons, but not all. And the "not all" part is what counts. I wasn't happy at my job. So, I quit. I can't tell you how much happier I am now that I did.

One time in therapy my therapist gave me a list of *100 things to do to make you happy*. The only way to truly be happy is if you are happy with yourself. Therapy 101. Been there, done that. But this list, it's the perfect list for my life lesson #3. If you do one thing every day to live it as if it were your last, it's bound to bring you some joy. They don't have to be crazy things. Go for a walk, plant a garden, pull out your CDs from the '90s and jam out, start watching a new TV series, call that friend you haven't talked to in ages, go on a date, plan a trip, actually go on the trip, and the list goes on. Basically, if you're waiting around to do something, don't. Because you just never know. Eat the cake, buy the shoes, take the trip. Life is short. And it can end in an instant.

Be conscious about how you live your life. Live in the moment. Laugh uncontrollably at anything and everything. Do something you love each and every day. There's that favorite cliché quote of mine again, *Live, Laugh, Love*. But is it really cliché? Or is it what we all should live by?

Chapter 48
Life Lesson #4

Let shit go. Just let it go.

Again, easier said than done. I have had to let a lot of shit go over the past ten years. It hasn't been easy, but holding grudges doesn't get you anywhere. Letting shit go has a wide range of meanings. From the little things, like how D dumps all the clean silverware in the silverware drawer rather than putting the utensils in their designated spots, to the huge things, like Shithead being found incompetent. Letting shit go is difficult because it is driven by our need to control. Being in control is not always worth it, though. Letting shit go enables freedom to do and care for the things that really matter in life. We can't control everything, and we shouldn't try to.

A current example of this in my life is when D is by himself with the kiddos. I will try my hardest not to "parent from afar," i.e., parent when I am not physically there. As hard as it is not to try and make sure every detail is tended to, or that some disaster doesn't happen in my absence, I consciously relinquish control, therefore allowing myself to enjoy my time away. I attribute a lot of my ability to do this to my case. Every day, I had to let it go that there was radio silence from the justice system. That I couldn't know everything right as it was discovered. That I was just a statistic in the jurisdictional game. Letting shit go is not for the faint of heart. I still struggle with it from time to time. You have to work and work hard at it.

Chapter 49
Life Lesson #5

Forgiveness. This word holds a lot of weight. After the rape, I felt worthless and responsible for what Shithead did. Forgiveness was not anywhere in my realm of thought. In the years following, I slowly learned how to forgive myself. And once I did, that weight became lighter. Holding on to the self-hatred and guilt paralyzed me. I couldn't move forward because I was still so angry. I realized that forgiving myself did not mean forgetting. I wasn't letting Shithead off the hook by forgiving myself. I was allowing myself to get better, to move beyond the rape, to continue living my life.

Forgiveness is one of the hardest acts to achieve, and it does not happen all at once. My forgiveness of Shithead, of Detective Dickheads, of the justice system, is still a work in progress. I have forgiven them to a certain degree, but I can't say I will ever fully. And I am okay with that. The most important person to forgive in this process was myself, and I did. There is no sense in beating yourself up if you can't forgive those around you. Once you forgive yourself, however, it brings peace. Peace brings happiness. And happiness brings the will to live.

Chapter 50
Everyone Needs a Mom

My mom is singlehandedly the strongest woman I know. I am the person I am today because of her. She guided me, befriended me, parented me, and supported me, all while getting shit done in her own life and raising another kid, mostly as a single parent. Everyone needs a mom. It doesn't have to be a biological mom. It can be a close family friend, an aunt, or a neighbor, but everyone needs a mom. Someone who gives you her shoulder to cry on, who picks you up after you've fallen for the 100th time, gives you a big hug after your team lost the big game. A mom who cheers with you when you get into college, who answers the phone at midnight and screams when you pass your CPA exam, and who holds your hand in the delivery room, should you beg her to stay.

My mom now jokes with me that I never gave her any stress until my twenties. We made it through the high school years, learning to drive, a few boyfriends, graduating college, getting a job, and just when I was ready to fly the coop, *bam*, the rape happened. Somehow, my mom stayed strong for me every step of the way. She always knew the right thing to say, or not say, when to listen or provide advice, when to be my friend versus a parent, and to always keep penuche fudge ingredients on hand. Being a mother now, I really don't know how she did that. If something ever happened to one of my babies, I would lose my mind. She probably did, but she never let on that she did. And not once did she ever make me feel ashamed about the rape. She fought for me and with me, every step of the way. Everyone needs a mom like that.

My mom is one of my best friends. She's also just a cool person. For her 50th birthday, she decided to go wild and do something out of her comfort zone. She got a tattoo. And not just any tattoo, a matching tattoo to mine. Now that is cool. We went together to that grungy tattoo parlor I went to a few years prior, and she got an enlarged woman symbol in the exact same spot on her right shoulder blade. She got different words for the circle, which read: Hope, Humor, Heal. If that isn't cool, I don't know what is.

We talk about everything from a cool rug that we saw in a magazine, to the latest on People.com, to relationship and parenting advice. We put it all out there, no judgment, and tons of laughing, crying, whatever. She is my biggest cheerleader and supporter. She is always there, and I know she always will be.

Chapter 51
Everyone Needs a Bestie

Bestie is one of a kind. We met our freshman year in college and never looked back. Going on fifteen years, we know each other like the backs of our hands. Everyone needs a person like that in their lives—a person who does not judge you, offers advice when you ask for it, listens when no one else will, and will take your secrets to the grave. A person who you can call anytime, has your back even when you might be wrong, and loves your kids like they are her own. Like D and my mom, Bestie played a pivotal role in getting me through the worst years of my life. She was that safe person who I knew wouldn't leave me, so she saw the darkest of my days. She stepped up to a job that a best friend should never have to do. And she nailed it.

When you can grow up (most of my growing up took place in my twenties) with someone and both change as people, but the friendship stays the same, it is rare. It's one of life's precious gems that I treasure deeply. We were the maid and matron of honor in each other's weddings. We have cried together, laughed together, traveled together, and have babies that are less than a month apart. I honestly do not know where I would be today without her.

Chapter 52
Everyone Needs a D

⌒•••••⌒

D is my rock. We tend to hurt the ones we love, and boy did I do a number on D. It was never my intention, but he was always my outlet. I couldn't yell at Shithead, so I would yell at D. I think he got the brunt of it because deep down I knew he wasn't going to leave. He probably wanted to, hundreds of times. But he didn't. We all need a person in our lives who stays by our side through thick and thin. D and I weren't together when the rape actually happened. But he was there to pick up the pieces and help me turn my life around. I am forever grateful for that.

When you find the person you are meant to be with for the rest of your life, hold onto them. Tight. You may not know it at the time, but it could be the dweeby kid you met on the back of the school bus. Through D, I found myself again. I became my own person, and he allowed me to do that. We have built this life together that is like no other. We go on dates, we reminisce about our pre-children lives, we talk about how fun and crazy post-children life is, we binge-watch Netflix shows on Saturday nights, we sit in silence on our phones to catch our breath after bedtime. We laugh, we fight, we get on each other's nerves, we co-parent, we yell, we have pillow talk, we grow, we have setbacks, we encourage each other, and we move forward again.

Chapter 53
The Other Side

June 29, 2008 made me a victim. Over the past decade, I made myself a survivor. It's not something I would wish on anyone, but damn am I thankful for what I learned and for where I am now: on the other side. Today, D and I live with our two boys in our lovely house in the cul-de-sac. We have been married for almost seven years, with many more to come. I am happily retired, for now, and staying at home with our youngest. Our amazing families live close by. We have a wonderful group of friends and neighbors. We are truly loved. I still take medicine for depression and anxiety; however, it has drastically improved and is more manageable than it used to be. I see my psychiatrist regularly and my therapist as needed. I still love scrapbooking and taking pictures of my kids. Seriously, I think I have taken a million since 2015. I'm that mom who goes big on holidays with all the outfits and props. Gotta get the picture or it didn't happen, right?

I ended up getting two more tattoos. I got the second one shortly after D and I married. It is a small Venus symbol on my left wrist, to echo the larger one on my back. It symbolizes how strongly I feel about women's rights and not being silent. It's a conversation piece for sure, which was my intent. I get all types of questions and comments, ranging from "Wow, I really love your tattoo. What is it?" to "Why did you choose the woman symbol? What exactly does it mean to you?" I prefer questions like the latter. I try to brush off the ignorance, as hard as that is, and simply explain my passion for women's rights. Some are probably sorry they even asked. I tend to go deep in my explanation. But, hopefully, it leaves them thinking.

My third tattoo is my favorite. It is on my right wrist, keeping with the theme of conversation starters. This tattoo is of the word *Survivor*, with the *i* being a semicolon instead of the letter. I got it on my thirtieth birthday. The coolest thing about it is that every letter but the semicolon is in ice-blue ink. The semicolon is in black ink. From afar, it looks as if there is only a semicolon there, but once you get up close, you can see the full word. I took a while to create this one. The semicolon means my story is never over. It is ever evolving and changing with me. I control the rest of it.

I live for Starbucks lattes, despite them once being tainted, and I also love trying out new coffee shops around town, by myself or with company. Nothing is better than lying on the couch on a rainy day and turning on a Lifetime movie. The same predictable storylines remain, and so does the accuracy with regard to sexual assaults. Perhaps others have found them as helpful as I did. I still watch my back, though I cannot think of the last time I was out and about past ten o'clock at night now that I have children. I rarely take a cab or an Uber by myself—only if I absolutely have to.

I love taking my three-year-old to his swim lesson on the weekends. He wears his goggles over his shaggy, curly mop of hair and gives me thumbs up every time he goes underwater. After lessons, we have a date at the Dunkin' Donuts down the street from our house to enjoy "the big one with the sprinkles" and "Mama's iced watte" (he currently has difficulty pronouncing *L*s). Our baby's unbridled giggles instantly put smiles on our faces.

I hate to cook; fortunately, D enjoys it, or else we would eat scrambled eggs and mac and cheese every night. I also strongly dislike reading books. Ironic, right? I have made it my New Year's resolution several years in a row to read three books in a year. Yes, that's right. A year. While some whiz through a good book in a few days, I'm over here pushing myself to read a few pages a week. I have absolutely zero patience for puzzles. The thought of spending hours searching for that one magic piece is nauseating to me.

I still wear my maternity leggings even though I am not pregnant. Long sleeved T-shirts are my jam, but I also love getting fancy and blow-drying my hair, putting on some makeup, and going out to a nice dinner every once in a while. I like to clean. It's a control thing. Vacuuming gives me a sick sense of pleasure, and nothing feels better than being done with all the laundry. Organization is bliss. I love purging, too. I'll take a big trash bag and walk through my house, opening drawers and closets, dumping items we don't need. I still occasionally eat an entire pint of Ben and Jerry's in one sitting. Not because my life is in dire straits, but because I can. Cinnamon Buns is my absolute favorite flavor. Depending on whom you ask, I am slightly better at sharing.

Reality TV is my guilty pleasure—*The Bachelor* is at the top of my list. It's so packed with drama that I can't stop watching. D and I love going on date nights and walking up to our little neighborhood bottle shop. I still drink, but it's much more under control now. Drunk Rachael will occasionally make an appearance, but in a different form, which is a major improvement. I love a good kitchen dance party and grilling out with the neighbors while watching all the kids run around. Some could even say our life is boring at times. That's something I never would have thought I'd be so happy about.

I occasionally think about contacting Shithead. The address of his jail is public record on the Virginia police department website. Just sending him a letter or something, to update him on yours truly. I do check every so often to make sure he is indeed still *INCARCERATED*, as it says on his inmate page. I breathe a sigh of relief each time I see that word screaming at me in all caps. Even though I was told I would receive a call should he ever be released, I still check. I do wonder what I would write in a potential letter to him. I said pretty much all I needed to say that day in court. Perhaps I will send him a copy of this memoir. He is the basis on which I wrote this, after all.

There are bumps in the road for sure. Marriage is wonderful but takes work, and parenting is full of joy, but it's hard. D and I fight and have arguments, and sometimes we find ourselves in particularly difficult seasons of life. Family members have gotten sick and had surgeries. Close friends have drifted apart. But I have so many tools and people I know to assist me in getting over these bumps and through the tough seasons. For the first time in my adult life, I am experiencing periods of contentment, where I am not wanting something to end or begin. Where I don't want more or wish for something different. Sure, life gets crazy again from time to time, and that contentment dwindles. But I work hard to get back to that ideal space. And when I'm there, it's glorious.

I have dreams and plans for the future. The future used to be unstable—nonexistent, even. It was a day-to-day existence for a while, but now I have dreams. I want to make a difference, both within my family and for humankind. I want to be heavily involved in my kids' schools and would love to be a room mom alongside teachers. I want to help plan the parties, chaperone field trips, get supplies for the teachers. It may sound silly, but it is my dream. My mom was a single mother who worked full time, and I wouldn't change my childhood for a second, but when my little brother was born and my mom took a year off work, she attended everything at my school, and I absolutely loved it. She always told me if she could have stayed home full time, she would have. And I now have that opportunity, so I am embracing it.

From a humankind standpoint, it seems like every time we turn on the news, there is another rape case to be solved, another predator on the loose. These stories are happening locally, nationally, and globally, and it's heartbreaking. My hope is for my story to change that at least a little. If my journey can help reduce the number of horrific attacks we see by just one, I will feel I have done my part. It's not only about raising awareness, which is critically important; it's also about prevention, what to do, and how to cope with the aftermath. My case could have gone in an untold number of different directions, but it ended the way it did, and I had to deal with that the best I knew how. Changing one person's life, one person's path, one person's will to live, would allow me my dream of making a difference.

Life is a funny thing. One day, you are about to die. And the next, you're living. Living this beautiful life. Somehow, I managed to take something awful and turn it into something productive, something hopeful, and something beautiful. *I* did that. Shithead may not have taken my life that night, but *I* am the one who decided to keep living. No one can ever take that strength from me, and if I can do it, anyone can. Trust me.

Tips from a Rape Survivor

If you plan on reporting a sexual assault, do your absolute best to preserve evidence for a rape kit. Don't brush your teeth, don't shower or even wash your hands, don't change your clothes. As gross as it is, all of these things will hopefully help in an investigation.

Reporting is scary. There is no pressure to report a rape. There are pros and cons to doing so. One of the pros being that a rapist can be caught. The cons, however, include a horrible experience with the justice system and not being believed, potentially putting yourself in more danger if the rapist has made threats about your reporting. I have no regrets in reporting. But I also completely understand those who choose not to.

Get STD tested whether you report or not.

Following a rape, get yourself to a safe place if possible. Regardless if the rapist is someone you know or not, go to a location that is unknown to that person.

Carry pepper spray.

Never blame yourself. You did not get raped. Someone raped you. Always refer to the rape as the action, not something that you received.

Fake it till you make. Do what you need to do to survive.

Be persistent. If you happen to have an experience like I did with the police, file a complaint. Don't give up just because someone doesn't believe you. A lot of people may not believe you. And as hard and shitty as that is, be persistent.

Make someone a knower. It only has to be one person.

Let people love you. It may seem easy to push everyone away. But try not to.

Go to therapy. One on one. Group. Whatever suits your needs. It may not seem like it will do anything. But I promise it will.

Take a deep breath. You will have the shittiest of shitty days. Maybe for a long, long time. On those days, stop and take a deep breath.

Believe in yourself. You can do this. It will absolutely not be easy, but you can get to the other side.

Let your voice be heard. Enough said.

Be aware of your surroundings constantly. If you feel like something isn't right, it probably isn't. Do your best to remove yourself from sketchy situations.

Always, always ask for help, even if you don't think you need it.

Your trust in others will return. There are good people in this world.

Try your hardest not to self-medicate. I drank. It was a short-term solution that ended up creating more problems.

Allow yourself to feel. Feel sad. Feel mad. Feel helpless. Feel frustrated. Feel happy. Have a bad day. Have a good day. All of it.

Once you're on the other side, enjoy it. Live each day like it is your last.

Thank You

I would like to take a moment to thank the incredible people who have helped me along this journey, and who have made this memoir possible. It is because of all of you that I am here today. My family and friends embraced me and took care of me in ways I never thought I would need. As the saying goes, it takes a village. Not just in raising a child, but through adulthood as well. Without my village, I would be lost.

To my husband, thank you for always believing in me and pushing me to do the impossible. You saw the good person in me when I didn't see anything in myself. And for that reason and so many more, I will forever love you.

To my precious baby boys, thank you for giving my life purpose. I am so proud of you and cannot wait to see the wonderful men you will become. Follow your dreams, follow your heart, follow your morals. Always have that zest for life, and always work hard, play hard. You both are my greatest accomplishments. Mama loves you more than you will ever know, to the moon and back and to the moon again.

To my mom, thank you for being both a parent and my best friend. Every day, I strive to be the mother you were and still are to me. Your strength, wisdom, support, and love have made me who I am today. You are the most amazing woman I know, and I love you so much.

About The Author

Rachael Brooks currently lives in Raleigh, North Carolina, with her husband and two children. Rachael graduated from the University of North Carolina at Chapel Hill with a Business Administration degree as well as her Masters in Accounting. She is a former Certified Public Accountant (CPA) who is now a stay-at-home mom. Rachael loves to travel when she can and also enjoys exploring her hometown of Raleigh. Strolling the Target aisles with her youngest, having impromptu cul-de-sac parties, watching college basketball, and frequenting the many different local coffee shops are among her favorite activities. Immediately impacted by the #MeToo movement in 2017, Rachael set out on her own personal mission to make her story known and join the thousands of courageous women and men who have also come forward to share their stories of survival and hope.

CPSIA information can be obtained
at www.ICGtesting.com
Printed in the USA
BVHW031037181119
564159BV00007B/116/P